MW01034420

Presented to:

_____

From:

_____

Date:

_____

THE
TRADING FLOORS

Discover the Power of
Trading in the Spirit

Published by Renaissance Publishing Group
(in partnership with)
Judy Coventry
For Worldwide Distribution
Printed in the United States
ISBN-10 978-0692258330
ISBN-13 0692258337

DEDICATION

This book is dedicated to my husband, my soul mate, and partner in life, Andy Coventry. Andy is the most loyal, self-sacrificing and kind person I know. Without his love and generous support of every kind, this book would not have been possible. You are my rock. I love you!

ACKNOWLEDGEMENTS

I would like to acknowledge the Holy Spirit, my Counselor, Teacher and Friend. Holy Spirit, thank You for the supernatural visitation while writing this book. I love YOU!

I would like to honor my Pastors and Apostolic Covering, Dr. Francis and Carmela Myles for opening the portal so that I could receive the revelation contained within the pages of this book.

I would like to thank Becky Chaille for the excellent job in editing the contents of every chapter and page. I could not have completed this without you!

I would like to thank my dear friend of seventeen years, Dr. Cathy Lowdermilk for co-editing and proofreading all its contents.

I would like to show great appreciation to Dr. Deborah Staires for her love and sacrifice in type-setting and formatting the book.

I would like to show appreciation to Kim Josar, Peggy Rogers and the members of Royal Priesthood Fellowship for standing with me in prayer for its completion.

I would like to thank Karen Hosey for offering generous love, support and expert advice throughout the process of publishing this book.

I would like to give a big thank-you to Nicole Faye Langenfeld for the beautiful artwork for the cover.

I would like to thank Dr. Bruce Cook, Pastor Mike Chaille, Dr. Luke Hall, Dr. Gordon Bradshaw and Danny Seay for their endorsements.

I would like to again thank Dr. Francis Myles, my friend and spiritual father for writing the Foreword.

ENDORSEMENTS

The Trading Floors adds a revelatory, insightful, powerful dimension to doing business God's way. Doing business God's way also involves doing business with the mind of Christ and the heart of God. We must not only be aware of and master earthly systems and processes, tools and weapons, but also be aware of and master heavenly systems and processes, tools and weapons. What Sun Tzu's *Art of War* is to military strategy and philosophy, *The Trading Floors* is to business strategy and philosophy.

Dr. Bruce Cook
Founder & CEO
Kingdom House Publishers

God's love for us is expressed in many ways. One of those ways is through "Divine Interceptions" in which He "takes us in" before Satan has an opportunity to "take us out." *The Trading Floors* is one of God's most powerful and strategic interceptions I have encountered in my many years of shepherding God's flock. Judy Coventry has taken biblical revelation along with personal revelation from Holy Spirit to offer the Body of Christ many keys necessary to keep us from trading life for death and blessings for curses. I highly recommend this book for every follower of Christ, especially those in the marketplace who find themselves on a "Trading Floor" every day.

Mike Chaille
Senior Pastor at *The Gathering House,* Powder Springs, Georgia
Co-Founder of *Firestarter Ministries International,* Hiram, Georgia

God's hand of blessing and anointing is upon the author and the writings of this book. This level of revelation is sought by many but only comes from intimacy with God. With the vast amount of challenges facing us in the twenty-first century, strong and authentic guidance is no longer an option, it's a necessity. If you can win on the Trading Floors, you will win in life.

Dr. Luke S. Hall, Senior Pastor
New Vision Christian Church
Forest Park, Georgia

> "See, I will send you the prophet Elijah before that great and dreadful day of the LORD comes. He will turn the hearts of the fathers to their children, and the hearts of the children to their fathers; or else I will come and strike the land with a curse."
>
> —Malachi 4:5-6

With this as my life verse, I have been overwhelmed by the presence of the "fathering spirit" that runs through the Order of Melchizedek and its implications for healing and restoration of lives. Judy Coventry so eloquently outlines the true Spirit of the Father and the counterfeit trinity of Baal, Jezebel and Asherah that has brought so much destruction to the family unit globally through "unholy trades," that many times we are not even aware of in our lives.

The uncovering of this demonic strategy and the antidote for reversing this trend is fully outlined in Chapter 9 of this book.

I believe this is a powerful picture of how the Trinity will bring restoration and healing to the "fatherless" through the Order of Melchizedek and heavenly strategies on how to make pure, holy and effective trades in the spiritual "stock exchange" which is headquartered in the throne room where Jesus Himself resides making intercession for us all continually.

This is a must-read for those looking to move beyond the anointing into His Presence, to operate in the Government of God for which we have been given authority and dominion to rule and reign as priests and kings forever in the Order of Melchizedek.

Danny W. Seay
Chief Executive Officer/CEO
Renaissance Marketing Group, LLC
G458 Holdings, LLC
Phoenix, AZ

"Every place whereon the soles of your feet
shall tread shall be yours…"
—Deuteronomy 11:24

Here is a powerful promise given to the children of Israel and a promise that still holds true today in principle and in practice. The "marketplace" is currently one of the most important subjects of discussion in the Kingdom of God and we cannot truly advance the Kingdom without having "soldiers" on the ground in the marketplace. The power of the Word and Spirit of God are being brought to bear in the marketplace today by courageous men and women who dare to "put their feet on the ground" and press into the conquest of new territory. In her book, *The Trading Floors*, Judy Coventry reaches into the heart of God for wisdom and powerful insights into some of the "gates" that are being held hostage by the enemy. She examines and expresses the supernatural methodology of God for taking back these crucial "gates" and securing them for the Kingdom. This is an excellent portrayal of what must be done today and how we, the kings and priests of the earth, must "tread on serpents and scorpions and over all the power of the enemy" to bring God's will to pass in the marketplace. This powerful book is an exciting read! Well done, Judy!

Dr. Gordon E. Bradshaw
President: *Global Effect Movers & Shakers Network* (GEMS)
www.gemsnetwork.org
Author: *Authority for Assignment – Releasing the Mantle*
of God's Government in the Marketplace

Contents

FOREWORD

Finally, a book arrives that changes everything...

It changes how we engage God, Satan and man on a common and shared platform called "The Trading Floors." The Trading Floors addressed in this book are "Supernatural Trading Floors," unlike the common stocks and bonds Trading Floors that animate the flow of goods and services in the marketplace. Nations cannot survive without the exchanges made on Trading Floors. The Trading Floors for the United States are located on Wall Street and the Chicago Mercantile Exchange. Multiplied billions of dollars are traded daily on these Trading Floors. In keeping with the volatility of all natural Trading Floors, people either make or lose money, and, in some cases, are met with financial ruin based upon how well or ill-advised they are concerning their trades on the Trading Floors.

The question that we must ask ourselves is simply this: If nations cannot survive without the trade conducted on Trading Floors, why would we think that the greatest Kingdom in the universe, the Kingdom of God, would not have Trading Floors? Revelation 18 tells us about the demonic city called Babylon the Great that is the mother of all abominations. According to the writer of the book of Revelation, the demonic kingdom is heavily invested in both the supernatural and natural Trading Floors. One of the items traded on demonic Trading Floors is the "souls" of men. Why would the devil be trading silver and gold with the merchants of the earth for the souls of men? It's because the devil knows the eternal worth of a soul. Jesus died on the cross to redeem our souls from eternal damnation. But because of man's greed and the love of money, the devil knows that most people will willingly trade their eternal destiny of salvation for temporary fame and fortune here on earth.

Hell is full of tormented souls wishing they could reverse the trades they made while here on earth. All too late they realize that the real exchange made on the Trading Floors was Heaven for hell! Unfortunately for them death seals all trades transacted on either divine or demonic Trading Floors.

In this groundbreaking book, my spiritual daughter, Judy Coventry has done the Body of Christ worldwide a great service. I prophesy that *The Trading Floors* will quickly become a must-read book for every member of the Body of Christ, especially for ministry and marketplace leaders whose decisions affect the masses. I highly recommend this powerful book.

Dr. Francis Myles
Author: *The Order of Melchizedek*
Senior Pastor: *Royal Priesthood Fellowship Church*
Tempe, Arizona

PREFACE

Why a Book Called *The Trading Floors*?

One day my Pastor, Dr. Francis Myles, asked me to receive an offering for a special ordination service. As I sought the Lord regarding the offering, I heard in my spirit, "The Trading Floors will be open this weekend." I didn't understand all that meant; however, as I received the offering I explained it the best I could from the very limited understanding I had received. The exhortation I released was very well received, especially by two of our guest speakers, one an apostle and the other a prophet. That same day Dr. Myles prophesied that I would write a book about *The Trading Floors*. I have to admit that I was in total unbelief because there was no way I had enough understanding of the subject to receive one more offering, let alone write a book. But what I didn't understand was that the Lord was about to take me on a supernatural journey. From that day forward the Lord began to teach me supernatural truths regarding trading in the spirit. I am writing this book to share what I've learned with the hope that your life will be transformed by the revelation contained within its pages.

I am not a theologian and this book is in no way meant to add to or take away from the sound doctrines taught in the Bible. I have never heard anyone speak or teach on spiritual Trading Floors nor have I ever read any literature on the subject. What I've written in this book came directly from the Holy Spirit during a seven week encounter. It is a "prophetic insight" as to how we trade in the spirit on a daily basis.

Definition of Trading Floor

A natural earthly Trading Floor is an area within an exchange or a bank or securities house where dealers trade in stocks or other securities.[1]

A spiritual Trading Floor is an area within the domain of a kingdom where traders can supernaturally buy and sell a diverse range of "kingdom stocks and other kingdom securities." The Kingdom of Light's Trading Floor is located in the third Heaven where God sits on His throne. The Kingdom of Darkness' Trading Floor is located in the second heaven where the principalities and rulers of this world reside.

Judy Coventry

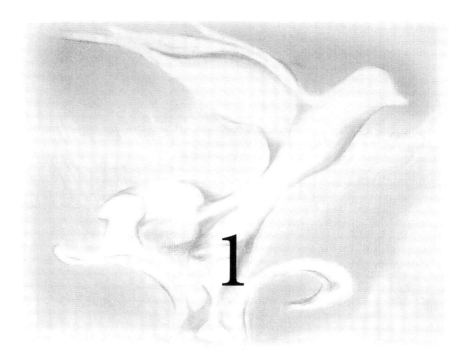

THE CLASH OF TWO KINGDOMS

The Bible is a history book about the clash of two kingdoms: The Kingdom of Light and the Kingdom of Darkness. The word "clash" as a noun means a violent confrontation. As a verb it means to meet and come into violent conflict.

The Kingdom of Light

The Kingdom of Light is owned by God the Father who is God Most High, Possessor of Heaven and Earth; His Son, the Lord Jesus Christ who sits at His right hand as King of Kings and Lord of Lords; and the Holy Spirit who is in the earth governing the Kingdom of God through God's sons and daughters, the Church of the Lord Jesus Christ. God's holy angels are also sent to assist us as we govern the earth.

But to which of the angels has He ever said, "Sɪᴛ ᴀᴛ Mʏ ʀɪɢʜᴛ ʜᴀɴᴅ, Uɴᴛɪʟ I ᴍᴀᴋᴇ Yᴏᴜʀ ᴇɴᴇᴍɪᴇs ᴀ ꜰᴏᴏᴛsᴛᴏᴏʟ ꜰᴏʀ Yᴏᴜʀ ꜰᴇᴇᴛ"? **Are they not all ministering spirits, sent out to render service for the sake of those who will inherit salvation?**
—Hebrews 1:13-14

God wanted to establish a Kingdom that would include many angelic hosts and many sons and daughters. But He did not want robots for subjects, so He gave everything He created a free will with freedom of choice. God wanted His creation to choose Him by an act of their own free will, so He created an opponent called Sin.

God's Opponent

The New American Standard version of The Open Bible capitalized Sin the first time it was mentioned in Scripture:

"If you do well, will not your countenance be lifted up? And if you do not do well, **Sin is crouching at the door; and its desire is for you, but you must master it."**
—Genesis 4:7

This is because Sin is an entity all on its own and Sin would have ownership of the opposing kingdom, the Kingdom of Darkness. This entity called Sin would be the exact opposite of the Creator God. In Sin there would be total darkness and no light would be found in it whatsoever. God is light and in Him there is no darkness at all.

This is the message we have heard from Him and announce to you, **that God is Light, and in Him there is no darkness at all.**
—1 John 1:5

Intellectual Property

Sin was given the right to establish a kingdom of its own. Sin would use darkness to come up with technology to establish and advance its kingdom. I call it the "Technology of Sin" or "Sin's Intellectual Property."

Intellectual Property (IP): The legally recognized exclusive rights to creations of the mind. Under Intellectual Property law, owners are granted certain exclusive rights to a variety of **intangible assets**, such as musical, literary, and artistic works; discoveries and inventions; and words, phrases, symbols, and designs.[1]

Sin's Intellectual Property would freely be used by all its governing agents, all the heavenly hosts that would serve it, and all the people who would serve it to help advance its dark kingdom. But those of the Kingdom of Light would not be allowed to use Sin's property, represented in Scripture by the Tree of the Knowledge of Good and Evil. In the day we eat of it we will surely die, because the wages of Sin is death (please note the word *wages*), but the free gift from God is eternal life (Romans 6:23). Eternal Life is represented by the Tree of Life in the Garden of Eden. The Tree of Life representing God's Kingdom is the only fruit of which we may freely eat; otherwise we will pay a price, a wage for eating from the other tree! Buyers beware! We will pay a wage for eating from the Tree of the Knowledge of Good and Evil that represents Sin's Intellectual Property.

As children of light we are only to use God's Intellectual Property to advance in His Kingdom. God's property includes, but is not limited to, the fruit of the Spirit from Galatians 5, the sevenfold ministry of the Spirit from Isaiah 11, faith and self-sacrifice.

Unrighteousness and deception are the foundation of the Kingdom of Darkness. Righteousness and truth are the foundation of the Kingdom of Light. Deception is the stock and trade of the

Kingdom of Darkness, and Sin "banks" on deception to advance its kingdom. Long before Adam and Eve were deceived in the Garden of Eden there was another who would be deceived by Sin and he would become known as the deceiver, the devil himself.

Ezekiel 28 explains the beginning of the fall of Lucifer, so let's look at the roots and origins of his fall.

> Again the word of the LORD came to me saying,
> "Son of man, take up a lamentation over the king
> of Tyre and say to him, 'Thus says the Lord God,
> "You had the seal of perfection,
> Full of wisdom and perfect in beauty.
>
> **"You were in Eden, the garden of God;**
> Every precious stone was your covering:
> The ruby, the topaz and the diamond;
> The beryl, the onyx and the jasper;
> The lapis lazuli, the turquoise and the emerald;
> And the gold, the workmanship of your settings
> and sockets, was in you.
> On the day that you were created
> They were prepared.
>
> "You were the anointed cherub who covers,
> And I placed you there.
> You were on the holy mountain of God;
> You walked in the midst of the stones of fire.
>
> "You were blameless in your ways
> From the day you were created
> **Until unrighteousness was found in you.**
>
> "By the abundance of your trade
> You were internally filled with violence,
> **And you sinned;**
> Therefore I have cast you as profane

From the mountain of God.
And I have destroyed you, O covering cherub,
From the midst of the stones of fire.

"Your heart was lifted up because of your beauty;
You corrupted your wisdom by
reason of your splendor.
I cast you to the ground;
I put you before kings,
That they may see you.
"By the multitude of your iniquities,
In the unrighteousness of your trade
You profaned your sanctuaries.
Therefore I have brought fire
from the midst of you;
It has consumed you,
And I have turned you to ashes on the earth
In the eyes of all who see you.

"All who know you among the peoples
Are appalled at you;
You have become terrified
And you will cease to be forever.""""
—Ezekiel 28:11-19

We know that eventually the devil will be destroyed forever in the lake of fire; but until then he is on the earth mastered by Sin. In Genesis 4:7, God told Cain that Sin's desire was to have him, but he had to master Sin. If we do not master Sin, then Sin will master us.

"If you do well, will not your countenance be lifted up? And if you do not do well, **Sin is crouching at the door; and its desire is for you, but you must master it**."
—Genesis 4:7

And do not go on presenting the members of your
body to sin as instruments of unrighteousness;
but present yourselves to God as those alive from
the dead and your members as instruments of
righteousness to God. **For sin shall not be master
over you, for you are not under law (Tree of the
Knowledge of Good and Evil) but under grace
(The Tree of Life).**

—Romans 6:13-14 (Emphasis added)

**…By what a man is overcome, by this he is
enslaved.**

—2 Peter 2:19

First to Eat the Forbidden Fruit

Holy Spirit gave me prophetic insight regarding the Tree of
the Knowledge of Good and Evil: I believe that Lucifer was the first
one to "eat" the forbidden fruit from the Tree of the Knowledge of
Good and Evil in the Garden of Eden. Sin soon became his master.
All of God's creations including His angelic hosts were told not to
partake of the Tree of the Knowledge of Good and Evil. That was
the test of loyalty for all of God's creation. Lucifer, the anointed
cherub who covered (Ezekiel 28:14) was the first to partake of the
tree. He partook of Sin's nature that day as he "ate" of the Tree
of the Knowledge of Good and Evil. Sin became his new master
and unrighteousness was found in him from that day forward.
The unrighteousness became so great he began to pollute the very
sanctuaries that he was supposed to cover with worship and praise
to God Most High. God had no choice but to cast him away from
His Presence because Lucifer was polluting everything with his
new sin nature. One third of the hosts of Heaven followed Lucifer
in his fall to deception and those hosts became the governing
force of the Kingdom of Darkness. Lucifer's name that means
light-bearer was changed to Satan, the accuser. He is known as
the prince of darkness to this day. The king of darkness is Sin,

Satan's master. Satan is bound forever to Sin because there is no redemption for angels. Angels do not have blood, and redemption only comes by blood for those with blood, mankind. So Satan and the fallen hosts are eternally bound by the chains of Sin. They can't get free no matter what they do as there is no redemption for them. Redemption belongs to mankind alone.

The Kingdom of Darkness

Sin is the king of darkness, Satan is the prince of darkness and the fallen angelic hosts, principalities, powers and rulers of darkness are the governing forces (the gates of hell) that manage the dark kingdom. The fallen angels have fallen celestial bodies. There are also demon spirits that do not have bodies and they are constantly trying to possess a body through which to express themselves. They are the lowest ranking forces in the Kingdom of Darkness.

The clash of two kingdoms, God's Kingdom of Light and Sin's Kingdom of Darkness, continues today! Which kingdom will you serve? Jesus said that we cannot serve two masters. We are either going to serve Righteousness or Sin. So the choice is still ours today. Choose this day, who will you serve? Joshua said, *"For me and my house we will serve the Lord."*

I choose the Kingdom of Light!

If you have never heard the message of salvation please refer to "A Note From the Author" at the back of the book. I would be honored to share God's plan of redemption with you!

LIFE APPLICATION SECTION

Memory Verse:

"And do not go on presenting the members of your body to sin as instruments of unrighteousness; but present yourselves to God as those alive from the dead and your members as instruments of righteousness to God. For sin shall not be master over you, for you are not under law but under grace."

—Romans 6:13-14

Reflections:

Who is the real king of darkness?

_____

_____

_____

What is the wages of sin?

_____

_____

_____

What is the free gift of God?

_____

_____

_____

JOURNAL YOUR THOUGHTS

As children of light we are only to use God's Intellectual Property to advance in His Kingdom.

2

LUCIFER'S FALL

On one occasion I was asked to receive an offering at one of our church conferences. By the Spirit of Revelation I knew that many of God's people were in financial bondage because they had been "trading" with the enemy and, therefore, he had legal right to access their blessings.

I went to my Bible to get confirmation from Scripture. This was the first time the Holy Spirit led me to Ezekiel 28 regarding the revelation of trading.

Unrighteous Trader

"By the abundance of your trade
You were internally filled with violence,

And you sinned;
Therefore I have cast you as profane
From the mountain of God.
And I have destroyed you, O covering cherub,
From the midst of the stones of fire."
—Ezekiel 28:16

**"By the multitude of your iniquities,
In the unrighteousness of your trade
You profaned your sanctuaries…"**
—Ezekiel 28:18

According to the above verses, Lucifer's fall came because he began to operate in unrighteous trade. The Hebrew transliteration for the word "trade" is *rekullah*, a noun that means "merchandise, traffic, trade." The primitive root is *rakal*, a verb that means "to go about, as a trafficker or trader." Lucifer had been trading while still serving as the anointed cherub that covers. This Scripture in Ezekiel is pointing to the dispensation of time before the fall of man because Lucifer was still on the holy mountain of God. So even before the fall, trade was a technology used in God's Kingdom. Without trade how would a kingdom be established or expanded? Trade is a very ancient technology that is still being used by both the Kingdom of Light and the Kingdom of Darkness.

Lucifer was attempting to advance his status in God's Kingdom by unrighteous trade. We know that above all things he was greedy for position. He wanted to be positioned above the stars and he wanted to be just like God Most High, as recorded in the book of Isaiah.

"How you have fallen from heaven,
O star of the morning, son of the dawn!
You have been cut down to the earth,
You who have weakened the nations!
But you said in your heart,
'I will ascend to heaven;

I will raise my throne above the stars of God,
And I will sit on the mount of assembly
In the recesses of the north.
'I will ascend above the heights of the clouds;
I will make myself like the Most High.'
"Nevertheless you will be thrust down to Sheol,
to the recesses of the pit.
"Those who see you will gaze at you,
They will ponder over you, saying,
'Is this the man who made the earth tremble,
Who shook kingdoms,
Who made the world like a wilderness
And overthrew its cities,
Who did not allow his prisoners to go home?'"
—Isaiah 14:12-17

Walking To and Fro

The Scripture states in Ezekiel 28:14 that Lucifer used to walk in the midst of the stones of fire. To *trade* means "to go to and fro." Today the devil is still walking. He is going to and fro in the earth attempting to advance the Kingdom of Darkness through unrighteous trade.

Let's look at the book of Job to see how Satan replied when God asked him what he was up to.

Again there was a day when the sons of God came to present themselves before the Lord, and Satan also came among them to present himself before the Lord. The Lord said to Satan, "Where have you come from?" Then Satan answered the Lord and said, "From roaming about on the earth and walking around on it."
—Job 2:1-2

The New Living Translation puts it this way:

> "Where have you come from?" The Lord asked
> Satan. Satan answered the Lord, **"I have been
> patrolling the earth, watching everything that's
> going on."**
>
> —Job 2:2

Satan is still patrolling (walking) the earth attempting to use deception on God's people to make unrighteous trade. He is watching everything that is going on, always looking for an opportunity to trade so he can accuse us of using Sin's technology. He enforces heavy wages on us for "licensing out" the Intellectual Property called Sin. The technology of Sin can bring many personal advantages and can even be very pleasurable to our flesh; otherwise, it would be very hard to market it as trade to advance the Kingdom of Darkness. The Scripture says Satan comes as an angel of light; so we must beware of the fact that he disguises his trade as something normal and good. His hidden agenda is always to advance the Kingdom of Darkness.

If sin didn't have its personal advantages or pleasures it wouldn't be tempting to use.

This is how the dark kingdom that Satan presides over advances with unrighteous trade and then by exacting wages from the children of light. This is now Satan's full-time job. No longer is he a light-bearer on the holy mountain of God. Sin "hired" him as the accuser of the brethren. The children of darkness can use Sin's technology as much and as often as they like because, after all, they are Satan's offspring, they are building his kingdom for him, and they are of no threat to him whatsoever. The brethren, the children of light, cannot "eat of this unrighteous fruit" lest we die (Genesis 3:3, 11). Of course we don't die right away, even as Adam and Eve didn't die right away, but the process of decay begins the day we partake of the unrighteous fruit called sin, until the day that we repent and apply the blood of the Lord Jesus Christ. The Lord Jesus Christ paid Sin's debt in full for us for all time and eternity!

We just have to apply His blood.

> Be of sober spirit, be on the alert. **Your adversary, the devil, prowls around like a roaring lion, seeking someone to devour.**
>
> —1 Peter 5:8

The word *prowl* means "to walk, to make one's way, progress; to make due use of opportunities."

The devil is always looking for ways to advance the kingdom he presides over by making due use of opportunities. What opportunities is he watching for? To trade with YOU! Be on the alert, he is looking for the opportunity to trade with you. He does not want you to advance the Kingdom of Light and if he can deceive you into trading technologies with him, he has won!

Satan Puts a Lien on Our Royalties

If Satan can deceive us into using the technology of Sin for advancement, then we owe him a wage (the wages of sin is death), for using his technology. He has made a trade with us and his kingdom advances while we are going bankrupt on unrighteous trade deals.

Satan puts a lien on our "royalties," our blessings that come from God, and we wonder why our prayers are not being answered. We wonder why we are not walking in the blessings of our father Abraham. And to top it off, the accuser comes back and accuses God before us. He tells us that God isn't who He said He is, that He doesn't really love us or that He is weak, etc. Oh yes, Satan is a master at accusing not only us, but he accuses God before us, as well. Anytime we hear accusations against God we must pull down those thoughts immediately because they are never ever true. They are from the ancient serpent, the devil himself. God is holy, He is perfect and all His ways are just and right. Justice and righteousness are the very foundations of His throne. He is absolute LOVE and God is always GOOD no matter what!

Our Father the Righteous Judge

God has taught His children how to increase and advance in His Kingdom by using His righteous trade technologies such as faith, love, sacrifice, the fruit of His Spirit, and others, but many of us are not seeing the increase. It is because the thief has stolen our blessings through unrighteous trade. If we've made a deal with the devil in unrighteous trade and owe him, then we owe him. God our Father is the Righteous Judge and any wages we owe Sin must be paid. The Bible says to agree with the accuser on the way to court; otherwise, we will stay in jail until we pay the very last cent. We must agree with the accusations that are being held against us in the courts of Heaven for using Sin's Intellectual Property. Many times Satan's accusations against us are true, and we must repent and apply the blood of Jesus to our sin in order to walk in the freedom that Jesus paid for us to have in this life. Again, Jesus paid the price for every one of our sins, for time and all eternity, but we have to appropriate the blood for it to be effective.

> "The **thief** comes only to steal and kill and
> destroy; I came that they may have life, and have it
> abundantly."
> —John 10:10

Many of God's children are living in bondage even though they live a righteous life and love God. It only takes one unrighteous trade to bring dire consequences as we will see in the next chapter, *How the Patriarch Traded*.

Our blessings are then held up in the second heaven on the Trading Floor of the Kingdom of Darkness. The good news is that in the Kingdom of Light under the Ancient Order of Melchizedek, the Eternal Priesthood of the Lord Jesus Christ, we can pursue, overtake and recover all our stolen goods from the Trading Floor of Darkness!

Light always prevails over darkness…always!

LIFE APPLICATION SECTION

Memory Verse:

"By the multitude of your iniquities, in the unrighteousness of your trade you profaned your sanctuaries…"

—Ezekiel 28:18

Reflections:

What caused Lucifer's fall?

_____

_____

_____

What is Satan doing on the earth?

_____

_____

_____

How do we advance in the Kingdom of God?

_____

_____

_____

The Trading Floors

JOURNAL YOUR THOUGHTS

_____

_____

_____

_____

_____

_____

_____

_____

_____

_____

_____

_____

_____

_____

_____

_____

_____

_____

_____

To trade means "to go to and fro." Today the devil is still walking. He is still going to and fro in the earth attempting to advance the Kingdom of Darkness through unrighteous trade.

How the Patriarch Traded

We are surrounded by a great cloud of witnesses and we can learn many spiritual truths from looking to the biblical accounts of their lives for guidance.

> **Therefore, since we have so great a cloud of witnesses surrounding us, let us also lay aside every encumbrance and the sin which so easily entangles us, and let us run with endurance the race that is set before us**, fixing our eyes on Jesus, the author and perfecter of faith, who for the joy set before Him endured the cross, despising the shame, and has sat down at the right hand of the throne of God.
>
> —Hebrews 12:1-2

As a matter of fact, the Lord instructs us to look to Abraham and Sarah:

"**Look to Abraham your father and to Sarah who gave birth to you in pain**; when he was but one I called him, then I blessed him and multiplied him."

—Isaiah 51:2

We can learn what to do and what NOT to do by looking to our earthly parents. So it is the same with our spiritual parents.

In the following biblical account of Abraham's life, let's look at what the patriarch of our faith did right and not so right.

Now the Lord said to Abram,

"Go forth from your country,
And from your relatives
And from your father's house,
To the land which I will show you;
And I will make you a great nation,
And I will bless you,
And make your name great;
And so you shall be a blessing;
And I will bless those who bless you,
And the one who curses you I will curse.
And in you all the families of the earth will be blessed."

So Abram went forth as the Lord had spoken to him; and Lot went with him.

Now Abram was seventy-five years old when he departed from Haran. Abram took Sarai his wife and Lot his nephew, and all their possessions which they had accumulated, and the persons which they had acquired in Haran, and they set out for the land of Canaan; thus they came to the land of Canaan. Abram passed through the land as far as the site of Shechem, to the oak of Moreh. Now the Canaanite was then in the land. The Lord appeared to Abram and said, "To your descendants I will give this land." So he built an altar there to the Lord who had appeared to him. Then he proceeded from there to the mountain on the east of Bethel, and pitched his tent, with Bethel on the west and Ai on the east; and there he built an altar to the Lord and called upon the name of the Lord. Abram journeyed on, continuing toward the Negev.

Now there was a famine in the land; so Abram went down to Egypt to sojourn there, for the famine was severe in the land.

—Genesis 12:1-10

Here we see that God reveals Himself to Abram with a promise of blessing. Abram is a new believer and, at this point, he probably doesn't even know God's name. The Lord tells him to go to the land that He would show him, which was to the Negev, the Southern part of Judah. God told him that He would make him into a great nation, bless him, and make his name great; that whoever blessed him He would bless, whoever cursed him He would curse and all the people in the earth would be blessed through him.

Abram gets to his destination and is faced with famine "in the land." In what land? The answer is the very land that God told him to go to. So what does Abram do? He heads right off to Egypt in the Northeastern part of Africa when God sent him to the Southern part of Judah. This would be just the first of many tests for Abram, because if he was going to become the "Father of Faith" he needed to "be" one before he actually "became" one. Get it? We need to already *be* before we publicly *become*. Well, Abram obviously failed this first test. I believe that if he had dug a well by faith where God told him to go, all his needs and his family's needs would have been met. For the lofty position of the Father of the Jewish and Christian faiths, God was going to have to work with a man of faith!

Dig a Well

So what lesson do we learn here? When we show up at the place where God tells us to go and there is famine in the land, we are not to go to Egypt (the world's system of Babylon). We are to dig a well right there! So how do we dig a well? The Bible says the children of Israel dug a well by singing to it.

Then Israel sang this song:
"Spring up, O well! Sing to it!
"The well, which the leaders sank,
Which the nobles of the people dug,
With the scepter and with their staffs."
—Numbers 21:17-18

In this passage *sing* means "to answer, speak, shout, to testify, to respond as a witness." We act as a witness by telling the situation what God has already said. We agree with the promise, speak it out loud and shout it into the airwaves! We overcome by the word of our testimony as we testify to the air! We shift the climate with the sound of our voices!

This passage then says they also used their scepters and their staffs. *Scepter* means "to decree, to govern, to inscribe." In the book of Job the Scripture instructs us to decree a thing and it will be established (Job 22:28). We not only speak, shout, answer and testify, but we also decree what the Word and the promise of God have already stated to be true. We decree God's word and the circumstances will line up with the promise!

We are also to use our staff. *Staff* means "to lean, to support oneself." We "lean on" our spiritual support system to help us through the famine. That is the support of our faith-filled friends and leaders. This is how we dig a well in the spirit when there is a famine!

Abram's son Isaac knew how to dig wells in famine. When there was a famine in Isaac's day the first thing God told him was DO NOT go to Egypt! He obeyed God, sojourned in the land and reaped a hundredfold that year. He also re-dug his father Abraham's wells.

Abram's Trade

By going to Egypt, Abram failed God's test of faith. Not only did he encounter a famine in the land, but he was suffering from a "famine of faith." This lack of faith led him down a path of fear and compromise. Abram feared that his wife's beauty might cost him his life, so he decided to lie to the inhabitants of Egypt and tell them Sarai was his sister. Right there we see a trade in the spirit. How do I know this is a trade? Because lying is a sin and it is a technology that belongs to the Kingdom of Darkness. It does not belong to the Kingdom of Light nor to Abram, God's chosen man of the hour!

The Intellectual Property of lying belongs to the domain of Sin. Sin came up with the technology of personal advancement through lying. That was not God's Intellectual Property nor is it ours to use. It belongs only to the domain of darkness. The Scripture says God cannot lie. Even if God wanted to lie, He could not because He is pure light. He is holy and true and there is no darkness in Him at all!

The Kingdom of Light's technology promotes ideas such as, "Buy the truth and sell it not"; "If you want to save your life you must lose it"; and *Husbands, go all out in your love for your wives, exactly as Christ did for the church—a love marked by giving, not getting*" (Ephesians 5:25, *Message*). Anytime we want to use a technology that is owned by the domain of darkness, we make a trade. Satan who stewards this realm under Sin demands payment. Abram is trading with darkness by lying. So what does He trade? Abram just traded his inheritance, the promised blessing. Ultimately, this is what Sin wants. The Kingdom of Darkness always wants our inheritance.

I believe the domain of Sin said to Abram, "Alright, you can use my technology called lying to preserve your life and I will take your promise of a great name. Instead of a great name, you will come out of Egypt branded as a coward and deceiver. And, oh yeah, the Lord said He would bless you. I will make sure you get blessed; you will come out with the blessing of Hagar the Egyptian. And, yes, the Lord said He would make you into a great nation. I will make sure you are made into a great nation; you will father the Ishmaelites. The Lord said He would bless those who bless you and curse those who curse you. Your own family will begin to quarrel and curse each other from now on. I will hold the promised blessing on my Trading Floor of darkness because you and I have just made an awesome trade in the spirit."

This was the reality of what happened that day. Abram had no idea he was trading his inheritance for the use of the technology of telling a lie. After all, Sarai really was his half-sister, so I am sure he justified the lie in his own mind; he was telling a half truth. Many of us in the Body of Christ justify telling little white lies or using other deceptive means to protect ourselves. But it is still a trade every time we use any dark technology. If we are going to inherit nations, we need to understand how trading in the spirit realm works, so we do not fall short like Abram fell short in Egypt.

The Kingdom of Darkness was advancing at Abram's expense. This was an awesome trade for Satan, and he was so pleased because he was profiting greatly on this unrighteous trade. He gets Abram's blessing and will store it on Sin's Trading Floor in the second heaven.

In His word to us God tells us to choose the blessing or the curse, life or death (Deuteronomy 30:19). The choices are always ours because God wanted all of His creation to have free will, freedom of choice. Abram chose the curse of lying, so the trade has been made. Because Abram chose the curse, Sin holds on to the real blessing on its Trading Floor and Satan stewards the inheritance of Abram, instead of Abram!

Do you understand how this works? The device of lying was not Abram's to use, but he used it. The device of lying for self-preservation does not come from the Kingdom of Light. In the Kingdom of Light if we want to live, we must die; if we want to save our lives, we must lose them. We can't use Satan's devices for free. He will gladly allow us to use his devices anytime. The more he sells his devices, the more he makes in trade. He is still greedy to make trade. He roams the earth night and day looking for opportunity to trade with God's chosen vessels! The more he gets to store up on his Trading Floor the happier he is! Remember what we read previously in Ezekiel 28? Satan was a trader of merchandise from the beginning. Beware! The greedy one has not changed. He is still in the trading business! He pushes his merchandise called *sin* as a means of trade.

So now on Sin's Trading Floor we see Abram's inheritance. Sin has it for now; but Abram is given another chance to prove himself a man of faith, worthy of the great inheritance as the "Father of Many Nations."

Another Chance

After this episode in Egypt, Abram and Lot separate because of the quarreling between their herdsmen. Abram gives Lot his choice of land and Abram takes what is left. After a while Abram gets a report that his nephew Lot and his family have been taken captive by four kings who had conquered five other kingdoms. Abram is faced with a decision: Do I act on what God promised me and conquer the kings who captured Lot with just my 318 men, or do I choose unbelief and fear again? This time Abram operated in faith. He believed God's promise of making his name great and blessing him, and with just 318 men he took down the four kings who had conquered the five kings, rescued his nephew Lot and recovered all of the goods. Can you imagine the spoil of nine kingdoms?

This was another test for Abram and on this one he got an A+. God gave him another opportunity to prove himself worthy of the title "Father of Many Nations." Aren't you glad for second, third, and fourth chances to fulfill destiny?

Abram Meets Melchizedek

This act of faith changed everything for Abram; it brought King Melchizedek of God Most High to the scene. (Jesus is High Priest forever in the Order of Melchizedek. I personally believe this was the Pre-incarnate Christ; see Psalm 110 and Hebrews 5-8. I highly recommend reading *The Order of Melchizedek* by Dr. Francis Myles for greater understanding of the subject.) If Abram had cowered in unbelief at this crossroad, do you think King Melchizedek would still have appeared? I truly believe it was this act of faith that brought Melchizedek to the scene. God was looking to make covenant with a man of faith. The man had to *be* before he was to *become*!

God had to work with a man of faith who could operate as both a king and a priest under the Order of Melchizedek. Abram had already shown God his willingness to act as a priest because he was already offering sacrifices in his daily walk with the Lord, but now he has also shown the Lord that he is ready to operate in the kingly dimension as well.

Quick Review

So let's review what we've learned in this chapter thus far: Melchizedek might have appeared before Abram went to Egypt if he would have just dug a well in the Negev as an act of faith.

Abram very well could have bypassed the entire journey to Egypt and a whole lot of trouble if he would have just believed what God said when He first appeared to him. Melchizedek couldn't show up until He knew He was working with a man of faith who could operate in both dimensions of priest and king. If Abram was going to be called the "Father of Faith" he had to prove himself worthy of the title. Abram had to *be* before he was to *become*. Wow, what a lesson for us to learn by looking to our Father Abraham!

Covenant with the King

This great majestic King Melchizedek is so impressed with Abram's act of faith that He now arrives to seal the promise with bread and wine, the sacred elements representing covenant with God Most High. This covenant act of receiving the bread and wine delivered Abram's goods from Sin's Trading Floor, because here we see Abram appropriating the blood for forgiveness and the bread for deliverance. Hebrews 4:3 says, *"His works were finished from the foundation of the world."* Jesus is the Lamb of God slain from the foundation of the world (Revelation 13:8). So it was a legal transaction in the courts of Heaven to appropriate the blood and bruised body of the Lord Jesus Christ in the day of Abraham, because in reality Jesus had already been slain.

This is the same way our goods are delivered from the Trading Floor of Darkness in our day – by repentance, appropriation of the blood and communion with God Most High!

This is the good news: All of our lost property and stolen goods are not gone; they are just being held up on the Trading Floor of Darkness. One of the supernatural blessings of the Order of Melchizedek is the recovery of lost goods. Jesus said, *"I've come to seek and save that which was lost"* (Luke 19:10). Under the Order of Melchizedek, what we've lost can come back to us. All of it! Plus interest!

Abraham recovered Lot and his family, plus the plunder of at least nine kingdoms. David was also operating under the eternal Order of Melchizedek (Psalm 110). After the raid at Ziklag, David pursued his enemy, overtook him and recovered all his lost property, plus all the property of the Amalekites and the Philistines, the nation the Amalekites had just plundered!

Once we understand how this works we will be prepared to plunder the enemy just like our forefathers who are now a part of the great cloud of witnesses. It is already in our DNA to pursue, overtake and recover all our lost property! We can go into the enemy's camp and take back what was stolen through unrighteous trade. We just need to appropriate the prophetic dimension of the bread and the wine of our Melchizedek, our King of Righteousness and Peace who is the Lord Jesus Christ!

Do you think Abram could really plunder nine kingdoms with just 318 men without the help of the Lord? Absolutely not, but his one step of faith brought the Lord to his side and the battle became the Lord's, not his!

This King Loves Faith

Even today when we step out without seeing, without knowing the outcome, and believe God no matter what we see, we become irresistible to our King because He loves faith. He will show up on the scene every time. Faith is what draws Him to us. Faith is the currency of the Kingdom of Light. When we operate in faith we also make big trades in the spirit to our advantage because faith is a technology of our Father in Heaven.

Faith is so much a part of the technology of the Kingdom of Light that Scripture says it is impossible to please God without it (Hebrews 11:6). As a matter of fact, the Scripture says in Romans 14:23 that whatever is not of faith is sin.

If we operate in faith and speak words of faith, then He will show up time and time again because He is the merciful and faithful High Priest of the confession of our faith. We must also be careful not to trade our inheritance with words or acts of doubt and fear.

Our confession is not in word only, but also in acts, because faith without works is dead. In other words, I will demonstrate my faith to you by my actions, and that is exactly what Abram did when he rescued Lot and his family. Right after this mighty act of faith, Melchizedek showed up and offered Abram bread and wine and said, "Blessed be Abram of God Most High." The unrighteous trade was redeemed by the supernatural bread and wine offered by King Melchizedek!

Blessing Restored

Let's look at what Melchizedek pronounced over Abram as they shared the bread and wine:

> **He blessed him and said, "Blessed be Abram of God Most High,** Possessor of heaven and earth; and blessed be God Most High, who has delivered your enemies into your hand."
> —Genesis 14:19-20

This was the first time Abram had heard the title of His God. He is God Most High. The same bread and wine that Melchizedek offered Abram will deliver our enemies into our hands and it will also shut down the engines of greed that would tempt us in unrighteous trade deals as Dr. Francis Myles teaches in his bestselling book, *The Order of Melchizedek.*

Abram just got his great name back! Instead of being known as a coward and a deceiver as he was when he left Egypt with Hagar, he is now known as "Abram of God Most High." He, essentially, is now the most powerful man on earth under the Order of Melchizedek, and a force to be reckoned with.

Abram's blessing has been redeemed by the body and blood of the Messiah.

King of Sodom Wants to Trade

Right after Abram meets Melchizedek and receives his deliverance, the king of Sodom shows up. What do you think he wants to do? You got it. He wants to trade with Abram!

> **The king of Sodom said to Abram, "Give the people to me and take the goods for yourself." Abram said to the king of Sodom, "I have sworn to the Lord God Most High, possessor of heaven and earth, that I will not take a thread or a sandal thong or anything that is yours, for fear you would say, 'I have made Abram rich.'** I will take nothing except what the young men have eaten, and the share of the men who went with me, Aner, Eshcol, and Mamre; let them take their share."
>
> —Genesis 14:21-24

Here, the king of Sodom, whose name means "son of evil," is offering Abram lots of goods in trade for people. Satan tries to get him to negotiate his rightful position before God Most High; he wants to trade with him again. "You take the goods and I'll take the people. Let's make a trade and be friends." But Abram had sworn total loyalty to King Melchizedek and was not about to trade on the Trading Floor of Sin again, as he had already done that once while in Egypt and it didn't work out well for him! Abram would not bow to the pressures or seductions of the enemy, which was yet another test that He passed. Abram was totally loyal to God Most High. No more compromise could be found in him. Communion with God Most High, the bread and the wine delivered Abram. He was a new creation!

Abram also became known as a man of truth who could not be bought and would no longer bow to the temptations of unrighteous trade.

> **For the eyes of the Lord run to and fro throughout the whole earth, to show Himself strong on behalf of those whose heart is loyal to Him.**
>
> —2 Chronicles 16:9

Let's see what happens next after Abram chose not to trade with the king of Sodom.

Abram's Compensation

> **After these things the word of the Lord came to Abram in a vision, saying, "Do not fear, Abram, I am a shield to you; Your reward shall be very great."** Abram said, "O Lord God, what will You give me, since I am childless, and the heir of my house is Eliezer of Damascus?" And Abram said, "Since You have given no offspring to me, one born in my house is my heir." Then behold, the word of the Lord came to him, saying, "This man will not be your heir; but one who will come forth from your own body, he shall be your heir." And He took him outside and said, **"Now look toward the heavens, and count the stars, if you are able to count them." And He said to him, "So shall your descendants be." Then he believed in the Lord; and He reckoned it to him as righteousness.**
>
> —Genesis 15:1-6

Abram's inheritance is now restored in full! And Abram also has righteousness accredited to him by his encounter with King Melchizedek, our King of Righteousness and Peace!

Let's look at this Scripture a bit further in the Amplified Bible:

> After these things, the word of the Lord came to Abram in a vision, saying, **Fear not, Abram, I am your Shield, your abundant compensation, and your reward shall be exceedingly great.**
>
> —Genesis 15:1

The Kingdom of Light has compensation for us when we use the technologies of faith and righteousness. God said Abram would be compensated and rewarded greatly!

> But just as it is written, **"Things which eye has not seen and ear has not heard, and which have not entered the heart of man, all that God has prepared for those who love Him."**
>
> —1 Corinthians 2:9

God compensates us for advancing in life through righteous trade. He is ready to compensate us with blessings that have not even entered our hearts! The problem is we have been involved in some unrighteous trade deals, so Sin has a lien on our compensation from God. Once we clear our record of debt to Sin with the blood of Jesus, nothing can stop us from receiving our compensation and great rewards from our Father in Heaven, God Most High, Possessor of Heaven and Earth. He possesses it all and He longs to give us the Kingdom. It is time for our inheritance to manifest on earth! There is absolutely no lack in the Kingdom of Light. Light always takes dominion over darkness!

Light Dominates

> In Him was life, and the life was the Light of men. **The Light shines in the darkness, and the darkness did not comprehend it.**
>
> —John 1:4-6

Let's look at the definition of two important words in this Scripture.

Light means "the power of understanding, especially moral and spiritual truth." *Comprehend* means "to lay hold of so as to make one's own, to obtain, and to attain to."

Once we walk in the Light and are illuminated by Truth and the understanding of the enemy's devices regarding unrighteous trade, he will no longer be able to make our blessings his own. He will no longer be able to lay hold of or obtain the compensation that belongs to us from our heavenly Father. He is going to have to let it all go because Light has come! Revelation has come! We now know the Truth and the Truth sets us free!

In Closing

We can always have what was lost recovered, but sometimes the consequences for using Sin's technology will stay with us for life. Such was the case with Abraham and Sarah. They, indeed, received their inheritance and became the father and mother of many nations, but the conflicts from their son Ishmael still remain to this day in the Arab nation.

God loves the Arab nation. It was never God's original intention to cast Ishmael out in the desert alone with his mother Hagar. But God in all His wisdom and foreknowledge understood that Ishmael and Isaac could not be raised in the same house. Ishmael had to depart because a son from Sarah was the promised inheritance.

> **So Abraham rose early in the morning and took bread and a skin of water and gave them to Hagar, putting them on her shoulder, and gave her the boy, and sent her away. And she departed and wandered about in the wilderness of Beersheba.**
>
> —Genesis 21:14

It was also never God's original intention for Ishmael to become a wild man against everyone, with everyone against him.

> Moreover, the angel of the Lord said to her,
> "I will greatly multiply your descendants so that
> they will be too many to count."
> The angel of the Lord said to her further,
> "Behold, you are with child,
> And you will bear a son;
> And you shall call his name Ishmael,
> Because the Lord has given heed to your affliction.
> **"He will be a wild donkey of a man,**
> **His hand will be against everyone,**
> **And everyone's hand will be against him;**
> And he will live to the east of all his brothers."
> Then she called the name of the Lord who spoke
> to her, "You are a God who sees"; for she said,
> **"Have I even remained alive here after seeing**
> **Him?"**
> —Genesis 16:10-13

God was so concerned for Hagar and her son Ishmael that He even allowed her to see Him! There are very few people in Scripture who were allowed to see God!

God knew the emotional pain Ishmael was going to have to face because of his father's unrighteous trade of accepting Hagar after lying to the inhabitants of Egypt. Can you imagine being Ishmael, and just as you are coming into your teenage years and your manhood, your father and mother (Sarah was Ishmael's mother by her maidservant Hagar) have another child who they favor so much more than you that they cast you into the desert to more or less die? Can you imagine the hurt and pain of a fourteen-year-old boy being cast into the desert by his parents after a new baby arrives? I cannot even imagine how he must have felt. No wonder he became a wild donkey of a man who was against everyone! He had a tremendous soul wound, and did not know how to deal with the emotional pain of his father and mother's abandonment and rejection. God knew how much pain Ishmael was going to face and that is why it was prophesied he would be a wild donkey of a man. God wants to release mercy not judgment towards Ishmael, the Arab nation. God knows that tremendous emotional pain is the root of their rebellion towards Him and the Israeli people. God wants them healed and delivered. God loves the Arab Nation and He wants us to love them as well.

God is love, He always was and He always will be LOVE. My friend, who is a Greek scholar, taught me that in Greek the word *agape* (love) means "generously concerned for." God was so generously concerned for Hagar and Ishmael that when they departed into the desert He spoke to Hagar personally. When they reached their darkest moment He made supernatural provision for them.

> When the water in the skin was used up, she left the boy under one of the bushes. Then she went and sat down opposite him, about a bowshot away, for she said, "Do not let me see the boy die." And she sat opposite him, and lifted up her voice and wept. **God heard the lad crying; and the angel of God called to Hagar from heaven** and said to her, "What is the matter with you, Hagar? Do not fear, for God has heard the voice of the lad where he is. Arise, lift up the lad, and hold him by the hand, for I will make a great nation of him." Then God opened her eyes and she saw a well of water; and she went and filled the skin with water and gave the lad a drink.
>
> —Genesis 21:15-19

We can see the love of God showing up on the side of the one who traded (Abram) and the victim of the unrighteous trade (Ishmael). Love is the greatest of all and love never fails. Even when we fail, His love will never fail us even in our darkest moments. Thank God for His unending, never failing, relentless love!

LIFE APPLICATION SECTION

Memory Verse:

After these things, the word of the Lord came to
Abram in a vision, saying, Fear not, Abram, I am
your Shield, your abundant compensation, and
your reward shall be exceedingly great.
—Genesis 15:1 AMP

Reflections:

How did the Patriarch trade?

_____

_____

_____

What delivered Abram's goods from the Trading Floor of Darkness?

_____

_____

_____

What Kingdom technology did Abram use to advance in God's
Kingdom?

_____

_____

_____

JOURNAL YOUR THOUGHTS

Even today when we step out without seeing, without knowing the outcome, and believe God no matter what we see, we become irresistible to our King, because He loves faith.

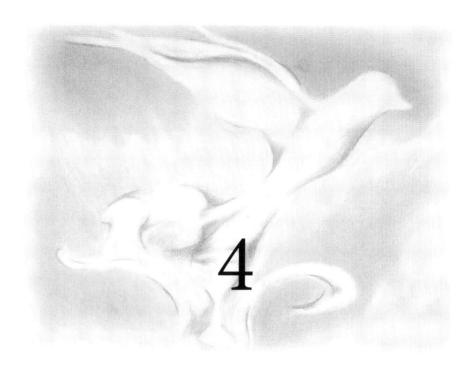

4

The King of Sodom and the End-Time Wealth Transfer

On the same day that Melchizedek appeared to Abram, the king of Sodom came and offered Abram a trade:

> The king of Sodom said to Abram, "**Give the people to me and take the goods for yourself.**" Abram said to the king of Sodom, "I have sworn to the Lord God Most High, possessor of heaven and earth, that I will not take a thread or a sandal thong or anything that is yours, for fear you would say, 'I have made Abram rich.'"
>
> —Genesis 14:21-23

The king of Sodom, whose name means "son of evil," is still trying to trade with God's covenant people, the seed of Abraham. The king of Sodom wanted the people. He cared much more about losing the people than losing the goods, so he offered Abram a trade. However, Abram had just met with King Melchizedek who was the King of Righteousness and Peace. He knew a trade with another king would cost him on the Trading Floors, so he refused the trade.

The War for Souls

The war today between the King of Righteousness and the Son of Evil is the same. It is over the people, lost souls.

Jesus' last words to the Church were, GO AFTER THE PEOPLE!

> **"Go therefore and make disciples of all the nations,** baptizing them in the name of the Father and the Son and the Holy Spirit."
> —Matthew 28:19

Jesus said that the gospel of the Kingdom must be preached to the whole world as a testimony to ALL the nations before the end would come (Matthew 24:14). We all know this war of the kingdoms is over the lost souls of men, women and children. That is the main reason why there is such a war over the mountain of finance in the Church. Without finances we cannot evangelize the world. Satan does not care as much about losing the goods, as he cares about losing the people. He knows and understands that it takes wealth to preach the gospel to all the nations, and that is why he fights us so hard in the area of finances. But don't be dismayed! God is fighting for us, He is on our side! Satan may have won a few battles, but the Lord Jesus Christ has already won the war!

Trading with the King of Sodom

The enemy has designed a technology to keep the people of God in financial bondage: Deceive the Church into trading with the king of Sodom—and it has been working. In doing this, he has legal accusation against the Church in the courts of Heaven. Satan can legally stop the end-time transfer of wealth because the Church has been using his Intellectual Property called "the mismanagement of seed." He has put a lien on our property, called "the end-time wealth transfer."

One of the greatest sins committed by the people of Sodom was the mismanagement of seed. Seed is always supposed to be used to reproduce after its own kind (Genesis 1:11-12). The men of Sodom wasted their seed with unnatural sexual acts (Genesis 19:1-29).

Judah's son, Onan, was required to have relations with his sister-in-law, Tamar, to produce offspring for his brother Er. Instead, he wasted his seed on the ground because he knew the offspring would not be his. This one selfish act cost him everything. The Scripture says that God took his life (Genesis 38:1-11). Onan traded his seed, the seed that was supposed to reproduce life, for his very own life.

It will cost millions of dollars to disciple ALL the nations of the world, but Jesus commanded us to do it. He knew what it would cost and He is ready to provide the funding. He is the Priest of God Most High, Possessor of Heaven and Earth. God owns everything; there is no lack of funds in the Kingdom of God. However, before God can release the end-time transfer of wealth (Proverbs 13:22; Ecclesiastes 2:26; Job 27:13-17) that is supposed to be used to evangelize the world, we, the Church, must repent for trading with the king of Sodom!

Mismanaged Seed

Many church leaders, including those of megachurches, are mismanaging the financial seed that they are receiving. If Satan can't keep the finances from us, then he will tempt us to mismanage the finances we receive. Many leaders today are giving the king of Sodom the people and they are taking the goods! The financial seed that believers are sowing into the Kingdom of God is supposed to be used to evangelize and reproduce after its kind. The seed is supposed to be used to make disciples of all nations and to defend the widow and the orphan, which is pure and undefiled religion. But instead, many of today's church leaders are being beguiled into using the seed to buy more goods! They are building magnificent church buildings where they can proudly display their names; many live in extravagant homes and drive very expensive cars. Others parade around in the most expensive suits, jewelry and watches, while people whom God desperately loves are being trafficked by the king of Sodom in all the nations where we are supposed to be governing and making disciples!

We learned earlier in this book that Satan was a master trader from the beginning and he uses deception (the stock and trade of his kingdom) to manipulate us to trade with him. He is tempting us to trade the people for fancy goods!

> "You were blameless in your ways
> From the day you were created.
> Until unrighteousness was found in you.
> **"By the abundance of your trade**
> You were internally filled with violence,
> And you sinned;
> Therefore I have cast you as profane
> From the mountain of God.
> And I have destroyed you, O covering cherub,
> From the midst of the stones of fire."
> —Ezekiel 28:15-16

The word *trade* when used as a noun means "merchandise" when used as a verb it means "to traffic." Satan is filled internally with violence and he is mastered by the sin of greed. He was also a murderer from the beginning (John 8:44); he is so greedy for trade that it turns to violence and murder. He is obviously the one behind the human trafficking which has become an epidemic in all the nations in which we are supposed to be making disciples. We are the Church of the Lord Jesus Christ, we are a governing body and we are supposed to be governing the nations that God loves, but instead we are caught up with "other things."

Seek First the Kingdom

The Bible says to seek first the Kingdom of God and His righteousness and all the "other things" will be added to us. The other things are good and it is God's will for us to be blessed and enjoy nice material possessions, but not at the expense of lost souls. Especially the souls of women and children that are being perversely trafficked all around the world! It is a matter of priority.

Listen to what God spoke through the Prophet Ezekiel concerning Sodom:

> "Behold, this was the guilt of your sister Sodom:
> she and her daughters had arrogance, **abundant
> food and careless ease, but she did not help
> the poor and needy."**
> —Ezekiel 16:49

We think that sexual sin and perversion were God's major indictment against the city of Sodom, but He also charged them with another form of mismanaged seed. They were living in the lap of luxury—proud, gluttonous, and lazy, while ignoring the oppressed and the poor! That was God's foremost judgment against Sodom.

Woe to those of us in the Church who have an abundance of food and careless ease without reaching out to the poor and needy! I feel such strong personal conviction even as I am writing this.

Many believers do their part. They bring their tithes and offerings to the house of God, but the leaders aren't always doing the right thing with the financial seed that is being brought to His house. The seed is supposed to reproduce after its own kind.

This is the same case that is recorded in the book of Malachi 3 regarding the Levitical model for tithing which is obsolete now (Hebrews 8:13), but the principal remains the same. (I will explain more about the Levitical model for tithing in Chapter 8). God's people were bringing their tithes and offerings to the priests but the priests were not doing the right thing with what was being brought to the storehouse, so the entire nation ended up cursed. The Church is a nation and much of the Church is under a curse because of the mismanagement of seed by its "priests," the fivefold ministry leaders. The entire Church is held responsible for the actions of its leaders. If the passage in Malachi is not proof enough, then just look at America; how many of us have come under financial judgment because of the acts of our political leaders?

We self-righteously point the finger at the political leaders of the day for mismanaging our nation's finances, but how can we expect our national leaders to rise above the leaders of the Church of Jesus Christ? God holds the Church responsible for the condition of the nation. The Church has allowed the demonic gate of greed for material possessions to be opened over our nation. Only repentance and the blood of Jesus can overthrow the judgments and accusations that are being held against us in the courts of Heaven. I believe it will take a "few righteous leaders" who govern the Church of the Lord Jesus Christ to plead this case in the courts of Heaven and it will speedily bring our deliverance. Only governing leaders appointed by God can open and close gates over a nation.

Again in Isaiah 1 the Lord addresses the rulers and people of Judah and compares them to the rulers and people of Sodom and Gomorrah. His biggest complaint against them isn't sexual immorality; it is their disregard for the oppressed and needy. They refused to defend the orphan and plead for the widow.

> Learn to do good; seek justice, reprove the ruthless, **defend the orphan, plead for the widow**… Everyone loves a bribe and chases after rewards. **They do not defend the orphan, nor does the widow's plea come before them.**
> —Isaiah 1:17, 23

If God expected Judah and Sodom and Gomorrah to help the poor and needy and to defend the orphan and plead for the widow, how much more does He expect this from His own blood-bought Church?

> **Pure and undefiled religion** in the sight of our God and Father **is this: to visit orphans and widows in their distress,** and to keep oneself unstained by the world.
> —James 1:27

We are supposed to keep ourselves unstained by the world. The world seeks after "stuff." We, the Church, are supposed to seek after His righteousness and all the "stuff" will come to us.

God gives us the power to create wealth so His covenant can be established in the earth. What is the covenant? *"For God so loved the world that He gave His only son that whoever would believe in Him would not perish but have eternal life"* (John 3:16). The covenant was made through the death, burial and resurrection of the Lord Jesus Christ, represented by the bread and wine. His bruised body and shed blood was for the lost souls of men, not financial prosperity; although that is part of the covenant He made with Abraham, which is still ours today. The "order of first things" in His Kingdom is the souls of men, women and children.

It really is God's will for us to prosper and to have nice things. My husband and I have a dream from God to own a beautiful home on a mountain in Arizona. The dream came from God, but we have come to realize that seeking first His Kingdom and His righteousness includes giving alms to orphans, widows and the poor. In this new season it just isn't going to be enough to bring our tithes and offerings to the church and go on our merry way. The poor must be considered and must become a priority for those of us who will inherit the end-time wealth transfer.

The same bread and wine that Melchizedek presented to Abram in the Valley of Kings is supposed to shut down the engines of greed within us, so that we won't be beguiled by the king of Sodom into forsaking the lost souls of men for the trade of material goods.

Mercy Triumphs

Jehoshaphat removed the remaining Sodomites in his day. His name means *Jehovah has judged*.

God is the Righteous Judge and the sin of mismanaged seed is already being judged, and will be judged further if we do not repent and ask for mercy. The Bible says that mercy triumphs over judgment (James 2:13). God wants to purge this sin, so the Church will be in legal position to receive the end-time harvest of finances, in order to receive the end-time harvest of souls. It's His desire that all nations who are called by His Name come to the house of the Lord. Jesus' greatest desire is that NONE would perish!

The problem is the king of Sodom has been manifesting in the Church, which has given Satan the legal right to withhold our supernatural provision because we have been trading with him. The Church has been using his Intellectual Property (the sin of mismanagement of seed), so he is demanding payment in full. He has put a lien against our property called the "end-time wealth transfer." Much of the Church has been plundered and is in financial bondage because of it.

The Bible says to agree with the adversary on the way to court; otherwise, we will stay in jail (bound up) until every cent is paid! Satan is the accuser of the brethren; his name literally means "accuser." He accuses us before God night and day. We overcome the accuser with the blood of the Lamb. The blood answers the demands of Satan for us and says, **"Sin's Debt Paid in Full, Redeemed by the Blood of the Lamb!"** Satan has no answer for the blood! He is silenced by it! We need to agree with the accuser because we have sinned. However, we have an Advocate, Christ Jesus the Lord, and He has justified us before God the Father. We must appropriate the blood of the Lamb to the unrepentant sin of mismanagement of seed and we will soon see the beginning of the wealth transfer.

> Then I heard a loud voice in heaven, saying, **"Now the salvation, and the power, and the kingdom of our God and the authority of His Christ have come, for the accuser of our brethren has been thrown down, he who accuses them before our God day and night."**
>
> —Revelation 12:10

Repentance is what throws the accuser down and brings the salvation and power of the Kingdom of our God! Legal accusations are the strong armor that the enemy trusts in. Once that armor is taken away from him we can then, and only then, plunder his goods. One stronger than him has come, the Lord Jesus Christ, who overcame the world and every temptation in it. He gave us His righteousness. We just have to apply what has already been won by the ONE!

Attack the Strong Man

> "When a strong man, fully armed, guards his own house, his possessions are undisturbed. But when someone stronger than he attacks him and overpowers him, **he takes away from him all his**

armor on which he had relied and distributes his plunder."

—Luke 11:21-22

It is time to attack the strong man and plunder his Trading Floor! Only repentance coupled with the blood of Jesus will bring the required force to overthrow the accuser so that we can plunder his Trading Floor!

"If I shut up the heavens so that there is no rain, or if I command the locust to devour the land, or if I send pestilence among My people, and My people who are called by **My name humble themselves and pray and seek My face and turn from their wicked ways, then I will hear from heaven, will forgive their sin and will heal their land."**

—2 Chronicles 7:13-14

For it is time for judgment to begin with the household of God; and if it begins with us first, what will be the outcome for those who do not obey the gospel of God?

—1 Peter 4:17

The good news for us is that there is a promise of redemption in Isaiah 1 following God's judgment on Judah in relation to the widow and orphan. I recommend that you take the time to read the entire chapter in context.

"Learn to do good;
Seek justice,
Reprove the ruthless,
Defend the orphan,
Plead for the widow.
"Come now, and let us reason together,"
Says the Lord,
"Though your sins are as scarlet,
They will be as white as snow;

Though they are red like crimson,
They will be like wool.
"If you consent and obey,
You will eat the best of the land."
—Isaiah 1:17-19

The enemy has been rejoicing because the Church has been deceived and living in darkness; however, the Lord is about to bring us out of the darkness. Our Advocate, Christ Jesus, is ready to plead our case for us if we ask Him to.

Do not rejoice over me, O my enemy.
Though I fall I will rise;
Though I dwell in darkness,
the Lord is a light for me.
I will bear the indignation of the Lord
Because I have sinned against Him,
Until He pleads my case and
executes justice for me.
He will bring me out to the light,
And I will see His righteousness.
—Micah 7:8-9

As we repent for the sin of mismanagement of seed, the Lord Jesus will plead our case for us as our High Priest and He will execute justice for us. He will bring us out to the light and we will see His righteousness!

Coming Prosperity

"Arise, shine; for your **ligh**t has come,
And the **glory** of the Lord has risen upon you."
—Isaiah 60:1

The word *glory* in the above verse means "abundance, riches, prosperity"!

"'As for the promise which I made you when you came out of Egypt, My Spirit is abiding in your midst; do not fear!' For thus says the Lord of hosts, **'Once more in a little while, I am going to shake the heavens and the earth, the sea also and the dry land. I will shake all the nations; and they will come with the wealth of all nations, and I will fill this house with glory,' says the Lord of hosts. 'The silver is Mine and the gold is Mine,' declares the Lord of hosts. 'The latter glory of this house will be greater than the former,' says the Lord of hosts, 'and in this place I will give peace,' declares the Lord of hosts."**
—Haggai 2:5-9

God is shaking everything that can be shaken. All the silver is His and all the gold is His! We are in the greatest day of the Church and now is the time of the latter glory!

Let's Pray

Heavenly Father, our Righteous Judge, we come before the courts in Heaven by the blood of the Lamb. We ask You to forgive us, the Church, for mismanagement of financial seed. We repent for not seeking first Your Kingdom. We repent for not bringing our tithes and offerings to the Church. We repent for the church leaders who have mismanaged the financial seed that has been brought to the Church. We ask you to forgive us for trading with the king of Sodom by focusing more on goods than on people.

We ask You to forgive us especially, and specifically, for ignoring widows, orphans and those being perversely trafficked by the king of Sodom. We repent for turning a blind eye to the atrocity of human trafficking that is rampant in nations of the world today. We agree with our accuser and say, yes, we are guilty before the courts of Heaven. We apply the blood of the Lord Jesus Christ to our sin. We appropriate the blood of the Lord Jesus Christ to the accusations that have been presented before You in this court case. We ask that the blood of Jesus would silence the accuser and that he would be thrown down. We ask that the power and the glory of the Lord Jesus Christ would now come to those of us who will steward faithfully the end-time wealth transfer. We ask You to raise up powerful church leaders who have hearts after Yours, those who will be a father to the fatherless and a "husband" to the widow. We ask for strategies to rescue lost souls and to save those who are enslaved in human trafficking. We ask for the grace to defend the orphan and to plead for the widow.

We ask You, Lord Jesus, to stand as our Advocate and present our case to the Righteous Judge. We thank you that Your throne is a Seat of Mercy and that mercy triumphs over judgment. Your word says that it is God who justifies. Therefore, who can bring a charge against God's elect (Romans 8:33)? We ask that Your blood would justify us before the courts of Heaven today. We ask that the Church's sin of the mismanagement of financial seed would be blotted out. Your Kingdom come. Your will be done, on earth as it is in Heaven!

Amen.

LIFE APPLICATION SECTION

Memory Verse:

"Arise, shine; for your light has come,
And the glory of the Lord has risen upon you."
—Isaiah 60:1

Reflections:

What was God's main indictment against Sodom?

_____

_____

_____

What is pure and undefiled religion?

_____

_____

_____

What does the word *glory* mean in Isaiah 60?

_____

_____

_____

JOURNAL YOUR THOUGHTS

Repentance is what throws the accuser down and brings the salvation and the power of the Kingdom of our God.

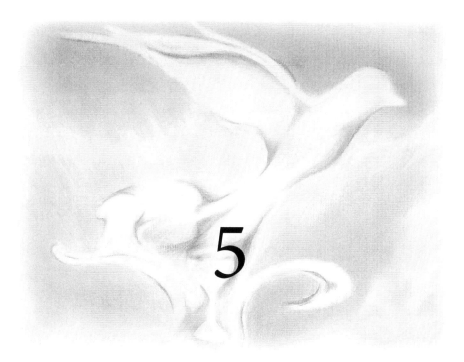

5

Trading at the Gates

If we are ever going to truly comprehend how we can cut our losses and make gains by trading, then we must first understand where trades take place. Most trades, whether righteous or unrighteous, transpire at the gates of our temples. Since we are the temple of the Holy Spirit, we have spiritual gates. This is where the majority of the trading in which we participate occurs. In Scripture gates symbolize strength, power and dominion.

Gates in Biblical Times

- News was exchanged at the gates
- Kings presided at the gates
- Prophets and priests delivered admonishments at the gates

- Reading of the Law took place at the gates
- Legal counsel was conducted at the gates
- Proclamations were made at the gates
- Business was transacted at the gates
- Legal transactions took place at the gates
- Justice and punishment were dispensed at the gates

Gates were potential weak points in the defense of a city and, therefore, became a matter of great concern during the time of war.[1]

If you reread the last four points referring to gates, you will quickly understand why most trade happens there. A trade is a transaction. When we trade in the spirit, a transaction takes place and it brings life or death, a blessing or a curse. It is also very important to note that the gates are always the potential weak point for entrance of the enemy and they must be heavily guarded.

New Gods Chosen

"In the days of Shamgar the son of Anath, in the days of Jael, the highways were deserted, and travelers went by roundabout ways. The peasantry ceased, they ceased in Israel, until I, Deborah, arose, until I arose, a mother in Israel. **New gods were chosen; then war was in the gates.** Not a shield or a spear was seen among forty thousand in Israel."

—Judges 5:6-8

The book of Judges was written in the "dark ages" of Israel. It was written in the time between Joshua's death and the time when Israel's kings were placed into office. Israel found herself in grave darkness during this time because Sin, the king of darkness, was crouching at the gates of the nation and the nation chose not to master it; instead, they gave way to it and allowed Sin within the

74

gates of the city. The Scripture says, "New gods were chosen; then war was in the gates." In other words, they traded with other gods at the gates of the city and it brought war in through the gates. They allowed idols in through the city gates, which brought the nation into a time of great distress and mourning. The highways were deserted from fear of the enemy; all singing, dancing and celebration ceased because war was in the gates of the city.

In Scripture the word *gate* is often used in a figurative sense. It frequently signifies the city. To possess the gate was to possess the city itself. Whoever has authority at the gates has authority inside the gates! Sin always wants to control the gates, so the domain of darkness can control everything inside them.

During the time of the book of Judges, the nation's leadership was very weak and the enemy knew if he could get Israel to trade with him at the gates he could then possess the entire nation.

Temple Gates

We, the Church, are a nation; we are also called the city of Zion. We each have a temple and are responsible to guard the gates of our temples. The gates of our temples include, but are not limited to, eye gates, ear gates, nose gates and mouth gates. There are other gates, but for the purpose of this chapter we will concentrate on these gates. What individual temples allow in through these gates will have direct effect on the City of Zion and the Nation of the Church. It all starts with individual gates and individual temples. That's you and me!

> "If you do well, will not your countenance be lifted up? And if you do not do well, **Sin is crouching at the door; its desire is for you, but you must master it.**"
>
> —Genesis 4:7

The definition of *door* is "an opening or entrance; a gate."

Sin is crouching at the gates waiting for an entrance. Sin is crouching like a lion waiting to pounce on its prey. It is waiting to trade with someone at the gates so it may have entrance!

Satan has a tremendous amount of merchandise available for trade. He has made this merchandise with Sin's Intellectual Properties of perversion, witchcraft, violence and lust, just to name a few. This merchandise is made available to trade for the souls of men. He has perverted media of every type, tainting it with lust, adultery and greed. It is readily available for trade through the eye and ear gates. But beware if you make a trade for this type of merchandise, as you may find yourself bound to it for life.

Addictive substances can enter through our mouth and nose gates. They may bring a temporary high, but that temporary high is frequently traded for a life of addiction and misery.

If Satan can get in through our gates he knows he will rule the entire temple and, eventually, the city and the nation.

Trading with Words

Jesus taught us that it's what comes out of a man that defiles him. If we allow darkness in through our gates, then darkness is eventually going to come out of our gates. The place it usually proceeds from is our mouths! If we are to put an end to trading with the enemy at the gates, then we have to, first and foremost, learn to master our tongues.

For we all stumble in many ways. If anyone does not stumble in what he says, he is a perfect man, able to bridle the whole body as well. Now if we put the bits into the horses' mouths so that they will obey us, we direct their entire body as well. Look at the ships also, though they are so great and are driven by strong winds, are still directed by a very small rudder wherever the inclination of the pilot desires. So also the tongue is a small part of the body, and yet it boasts of great things.

See how great a forest is set aflame by such a small fire! **And the tongue is a fire, the very world of iniquity; the tongue is set among our members as that which defiles the entire body, and sets on fire the course of our life, and is set on fire by hell.** For every species of beasts and birds, of reptiles and creatures of the sea, is tamed and has been tamed by the human race. **But no one can tame the tongue; it is a restless evil and full of deadly poison.** With it we bless our Lord and Father, and with it we curse men, who have been made in the likeness of God; from the same mouth come both blessing and cursing. My brethren, these things ought not to be this way.

—James 3:2-10

James, the Lord's brother, states that the way to be perfect is to master what we say. In other words, if we can master what comes out of our mouth gate we will be perfect. I wonder if he remembered what the Lord said as recorded in Matthew 5:48, "**Therefore you are to be perfect,** as your heavenly Father is perfect."

Jesus also warned us to guard our ear gates. He said, "*Take care what you listen to. By your standard of measure it will be measured to you; and more will be given you besides*" (Mark 4:24). What we hear can enter our hearts. Jesus also said that out of the abundance of our hearts our mouths would speak (Matthew 12:34).

What we allow in our souls through our eye and ear gates will eventually enter our hearts and come out through our mouths. It is critical that we guard our gates because they all are a point of entry to the soul, which leads to the heart. And out of the heart flow the very issues of life. I was once taught that the heart of man is the place where his spirit and soul connect. We must protect this vulnerable place of the heart by keeping a heavy guard over our gates. David, the only man mentioned as a man after God's own heart, understood this:

> May my prayer be counted as incense before You;
> The lifting up of my hands as the evening offering.
> **Set a guard, O Lord, over my mouth;**
> **Keep watch over the door of my lips.**
> **Do not incline my heart to any evil thing,**
> To practice deeds of wickedness
> With men who do iniquity;
> **And do not let me eat of their delicacies.**
> —Psalm 141:2-4

Words spoken or heard will incline our hearts one way or the other, towards good or evil. The delicacies David speaks of are the fruit that comes from the words of lips with unguarded doors. We are not to partake of them.

Proverbs 18:21 says, *"Death and life are in the **power of the tongue,** and those who love it will eat its fruit."* Words always produce a harvest of fruit, good or bad. We trade with our words and we are either going to harvest life or death depending on whose Intellectual Property we are using. If we are using the Kingdom of Light's words, then we will reap eternal life; if we are using the Kingdom of Darkness' words, then we are going to reap corruption. The word *power* in Proverbs 18:21 means "hand." Life and death are in the hand of the tongue! In America we use the phrase, "It's in your hands." In reality our lives are in the hand of our tongue and Sin knows it. It wants control of our lives, so it crouches at the door waiting to make a trade with our tongue! This is where the majority of trade happens, at the mouth gate!

We trade with our words every day; even marriage and business covenants are established or broken by words. Words have power!

Not only does the enemy try to get in through the gates, but he will tempt us to "peddle" his merchandise through our gates, as well, specifically the mouth gate! He will tempt us to use our mouth gate to distribute Sin's Intellectual Property called gossip, talebearing and accusation.

Let's look at the key Scripture from Ezekiel 28 again:

> **"By the abundance of your trade**
> **You were internally filled with violence,**
> **And you sinned;**
> Therefore I have cast you as profane
> From the mountain of God.
> And I have destroyed you, O covering cherub,
> From the midst of the stones of fire."
> —Ezekiel 28:16

The word *trade* not only has to do with merchandise, but also with talebearing and gossip. In Leviticus 19 the word *slanderer* **has the same meaning as the word** *trade* **in Ezekiel 28:16.**

> "You shall not go about as a **slanderer among your people,** and you are not to act against the life of your neighbor; I am the Lord."
> —Leviticus 19:16

In all probability Satan was peddling the merchandise called gossip. He was profaning the Lord's sanctuary with gossip and slander, and his mission is still the same today! One of the most prevalent ways we conduct trade is to trade with our words. Slander, gossip and accusations are enormous unrighteous trades in the spirit realm. When we use undermining words, especially to discount someone to make ourselves look better, then we've made a trade in the spirit. Gossip is an unrighteous trade. Even the most subtle forms of "church gossip," such as "We really need to pray for so and so because…," or "So and so really hurt my feelings because…," are unrighteous trades that need to be avoided at all costs, otherwise they will cost us on the Trading Floors!

Everything is heard in the realm of the spirit. God doesn't miss anything. He hears everything 100% of the time. God is omnipresent, everywhere all at once and He is not dull of hearing! If we choose gossip, no matter how we try to disguise it, He will hear it and it will cause us to lose stature before Him just as it cost Lucifer stature and position on the mount of God in the Garden of Eden. Satan, who is still roaming about the earth listening and watching, will also hear it and the accuser will use it as an unrighteous trade against us. Buyers, beware!

Proverbs 6 mentions seven things that the Lord hates and three of them have to do with talebearing and gossip! He hates a lying tongue, a false witness and one who spreads strife amongst the brethren. He hates these things! Satan lost his position on the Lord's holy mountain due to these very things. Now he wants us to lose our mountains the very same way he lost his.

The Accuser

We know that the devil's name was changed from Lucifer, the light-bearer, to Satan, the accuser. Satan's job is to accuse the Body of Christ before the throne of God night and day. He does everything in his power to get us to join him in his rebellion.

The Scripture says in Ephesians 2:6 that we are seated in heavenly places in Christ Jesus. Jesus said, *"I go to prepare a place for you...that where I am, there you may be also"* (John 14:3). In reality we live with Him in Zion. We are positioned before the throne of God in the courts of Heaven. Satan lost his position on the mount of God, so now he needs to use us to do his bidding for him. He manipulates us to traffic his merchandise of gossip and accusation in the sanctuary of God. He now uses us to accuse the brethren before the throne of God night and day. Haven't we observed this over and over in the Church? This is Satan's strategy to divide and conquer and render the Church powerless because power is manifested in unity of the brethren (Psalm 133).

Power is displayed through mercy, not judgment. Judgment has NO power. ALL power has been invested in mercy for the Body of Christ. Jesus sits on a throne called the Mercy Seat. When we accuse and judge one another we become powerless. God says that *mercy triumphs over judgment* (James 2:13). We are seated in heavenly places in Christ Jesus on a throne of mercy, not judgment.

God alone is the Righteous Judge and all judgment is for God alone. We are to discern and pray but not judge and accuse; otherwise, we will be trading with the king of darkness called Sin.

Sin wants us to trade with our mouths by gossiping and accusing our brothers and sisters in Christ. Sin understands that life and death are in the power of the tongue. Sin's kingdom has no power without our voice of agreement before the throne of God. It must have us agree with its lies and speak them out, and then it has power. Once we use its words, its lies and its accusations, "Sin's Intellectual Property," then we've made a trade in the spirit and we will eat its fruit! The fruit of Sin's words will always bring death, and that is why it is so important for us to master guarding this particular gate.

Jesus at the Gates

Sin is crouching at the door (gate), but guess what? Jesus is also at the door (gate).

> **"Behold, I stand at the door and knock;** if anyone
> hears My voice and opens the door, I will come in
> to him and will dine with him, and he with Me."
> —Revelation 3:20

Both Sin and Jesus want access to the door. Both kingdoms are warring over the door because whoever possesses the door (gate) will possess what's inside the door (gate).

> **Lift up your heads, O gates, and be lifted up, O
> ancient doors, that the King of glory may come**

in! Who is the King of glory? The Lord strong and mighty, the Lord mighty in battle. Lift up your heads, O gates, and lift them up, O ancient doors, that the King of glory may come in! Who is this King of glory? The Lord of hosts, He is the King of glory.

—Psalm 24:7-10

The main gates of entrance to our temples are attached to our heads. When we lift up our heads with intention of beholding Jesus, then He comes in through our gates. The Lord strong and mighty comes in through the gates!

We can trade at the gates with Jesus, as well:

"I advise you to buy from Me gold refined by fire so that you may become rich, and white garments so that you may clothe yourself, and that the shame of your nakedness will not be revealed; and eye salve to anoint your eyes so that you may see."

—Revelation 3:18

Possessing the Gates

It is our inheritance to not only control and possess our own gates, but we are also to possess the gates of our enemies.

"Indeed I will greatly bless you, and I will greatly multiply your seed as the stars of the heavens and as the sand which is on the seashore; **and your seed shall possess the gate of their enemies.**"

—Genesis 22:17

They blessed Rebekah and said to her, "May you, our sister, become thousands of ten thousands, and **may your descendants possess the gate of those who hate them.**"

—Genesis 24:60

God's promise to Abraham was then confirmed to Rebekah by her family as they sent her off to become Isaac's wife. Jesus said He became a curse so that the blessing of Abraham could come upon us. It is His divine will for us to possess gates and it is in our spiritual DNA to possess gates! If we can possess the gates, we can possess the city! But how can we possess the gates of our enemies if the enemy possesses ours? You are right; we can't. That is why there is constant war over the gates. Sin crouches at the door (gates) waiting to make a trade. Jesus stands at the door (gate) and gently knocks.

Samson, a judge who lived in the "dark ages" of Israel, traded with the Lord to have supernatural strength. He was a Nazarite and gave up (traded) his right to drink wine, touch anything dead, and cut his hair. The trade was ON. In trade for this Nazarite vow, God allowed him to possess the Spirit of Might. Let's look at one of the passages of Scripture from Samson's day:

> When it was told to the Gazites, saying, "Samson has come here," **they surrounded the place and lay in wait for him all night at the gate of the city.** And they kept silent all night, saying, "Let us wait until the morning light, then we will kill him." Now Samson lay until midnight, and at midnight **he arose and took hold of the doors of the city gate and the two posts and pulled them up along with the bars; then he put them on his shoulders and carried them up to the top of the mountain which is opposite Hebron."**
> —Judges 16:2-4

Do you see the prophetic picture here? The enemy is crouching at the gates to kill Samson. However, before this episode Samson had been trading in the spirit; he had completely consecrated himself to God as a Nazarite. So, when the time comes for war at the gates, Samson is able to pull the doors and bars of the city gate right up out of the ground and carry them to the top of the mountain on his shoulders!

That is exactly what God wants us to do in our day. Samson was consecrated to the Lord, so he was prepared not to trade with the enemy at the gates. He instead pulled up the doors of the city gate, put them on his shoulders and carried them up the mountain! God wants us to take the gates of cities and nations to the top of our mountains using the strength of His government that is upon our shoulders. It is in our DNA to possess gates. We see Samson fulfilling Abrahamic prophecy right here in this passage of Scripture from Judges 16.

The Spirit of Might is part of the government of God listed in Isaiah 11. It was the strength of God's government upon Samson's shoulders that allowed Samson to minister with such power and authority. When we consecrate ourselves to the Lord and only allow Him to enter through the gates, we get the King of Glory! And who is the King of Glory? The Lord strong and mighty, the Lord mighty in battle. This is how we receive the Spirit of Might!

Judges 16:3 says that Samson arose to save his nation from the enemy at the gates. In Judges 5:7 it states that Deborah also arose to save the nation of Israel while there was war in the gates. There is still war at the gates today in every nation and every city of the world. Where are the heroes of faith like Samson and Deborah? God is "raising up" His end-time army right now and we, too, will possess the gates of our enemies. It is in our DNA to do so! It's time for the Church to arise! The gates of hell will not prevail against us. In this day, we shall prevail against the gates of hell because greater is He that is within us than he that is in the world!

Crystal Gates

In conclusion to this chapter, let's visit the end of the story about Deborah and how she arose as a mother in Israel to deliver her nation when war was in the gates.

Now Deborah, a prophetess, the wife of
Lappidoth, was judging Israel at that time. **She
used to sit under the palm tree of Deborah
between Ramah and Bethel** in the hill country of
Ephraim; and the sons of Israel came up to her for
judgment. Now she sent and summoned Barak the
son of Abinoam from Kedesh-naphtali, and said
to him, "Behold, the Lord, the God of Israel, has
commanded, 'Go and march to Mount Tabor, and
take with you ten thousand men from the sons
of Naphtali and from the sons of Zebulun. I will
draw out to you Sisera, the commander of Jabin's
army, with his chariots and his many troops to the
river Kishon, and I will give him into your hand.'"
—Judges 4:4-7

Deborah was sitting under a palm tree between Ramah and
Bethel when she heard the command of the Lord for Barak, the
nation of Israel's military general. This one command would deliver
the entire nation of twenty years of tremendous sorrow.

Because Deborah had crystal clear "gates," she heard the word
of the Lord for the nation. Deborah traded time; she sat under the
palm tree, a date palm. Deborah had a "date" with the Lord every
day and she spent (traded) time listening to the Lord under the
tree. Her trade was time and her reward in trade was victory for
the entire nation for forty years afterwards. Deborah's name goes
down in history!

The Lord will give us "gates of crystal" if we pursue Him for
them.

"Moreover, I will make your battlements of rubies,
and your gates of crystal, and your entire wall of
precious stones."
—Isaiah 54:12

Battlements mean "daylight." Once our gates are secured for the Kingdom of Light, then we are going to have clarity and more daylight! We need daylight to battle effectively. Remember how Joshua told the sun to stand still because he needed more daylight to win the battle he was fighting (Joshua 10:12-13)? We need spiritual daylight so we can see clearly in the spirit realm to win every battle in which the Lord calls us to engage. Get ready because He wants to give us gates of crystal, so we can see and hear "crystal clear" every time He calls us to engage in battle.

Deborah sat under the "date" palm between Ramah and Bethel. Ramah means **hill** and Bethel was the place where Jacob encountered the **gate to Heaven** with angels ascending and descending. It means "house of God."

> **Who may ascend into the hill of the Lord?**
> And who may stand in His holy place?
> He who has clean hands and a pure heart,
> Who has not lifted up his soul to falsehood
> And has not sworn deceitfully.
> He shall receive a blessing from the Lord
> And righteousness from the God of his salvation.
> **This is the generation of those who seek Him,**
> **Who seek Your face—even Jacob. Selah.**
>
> **Lift up your heads, O gates,**
> **And be lifted up, O ancient doors,**
> **That the King of glory may come in!**
> —Psalm 24:3-7

Deborah had clean hands and a pure heart, she had not lifted her soul to falsehood and she had not sworn deceitfully. She was allowed to ascend the hill **(Ramah)** of the Lord. She received the blessing of the generation of those who seek His face, even Jacob **(Bethel/The GATEWAY to Heaven)**. The result was that the Lord strong and mighty came in through the gates!

Victory in the Gates

Deborah was able to "arise" and ascend the hill of the Lord because her gates were clear and her heart was pure. This connected her to the gates of Heaven. She found herself seated in heavenly places able to hear the Commander-in-Chief's voice. Deborah traded her time to access God's Presence on the holy hill. Because of that she was able to lead ten thousand soldiers to victory and save her nation, all because she heard the Commander's voice on the holy hill under the "date" palm.

Let's summarize how the nation of Israel experienced victory:

> "The peasantry ceased, they ceased in Israel, **until I, Deborah, arose, until I arose, a mother in Israel.**"
> —Judges 5:7

Deborah ascended the hill of the Lord called Ramah. She arose with the word of the Lord for the nation's army general, and people returned to the uninhabited city.

> "New gods were chosen; then war was in the gates. Not a shield or a spear was seen among forty thousand in Israel. My heart goes out to the commanders of Israel, the volunteers among the people; bless the Lord! **You who ride on white donkeys, you who sit on rich carpets, and you who travel on the road—sing!**"
> —Judges 5:8-10

Deborah brought singing back to the streets of the city again; they were no longer deserted.

> "At the sound of those who divide flocks among the watering places, there they shall recount the righteous deeds of the Lord, the righteous deeds for His peasantry in Israel. **Then the people of the**

Lord went down to the gates."

— Judges 5:11

There is activity at the city gates again, recounting the righteous deeds of the Lord; no more trading with other gods!

"Thus let all Your enemies perish, O Lord; **but let those who love Him be like the rising of the sun in its might."** And the land was undisturbed for forty years.

— Judges 5:31

The nation was able to rise in the Spirit of Might and enjoyed forty years of peace.

The King of Glory came into the city gates because one woman traded her time for His presence. After twenty years of war with the Canaanite King Jabin and his wicked military leader Sisera, they were able to enjoy twice as much time free from the ravages of war — forty years of peace and joy, all because of the consecration of one!

LIFE APPLICATION SECTION

Memory Verse:

Lift up your heads, O gates, and be lifted up, O ancient doors, that the King of glory may come in! Who is the King of glory? The Lord strong and mighty, the Lord mighty in battle.

—Psalm 24:7-8

Reflections:

The gates of our temple include, but are not limited to, which four gates?

_____

_____

_____

At what temple gate does most trade take place?

_____

_____

_____

Why was Deborah able to lead her nation to victory?

_____

_____

_____

The Trading Floors

JOURNAL YOUR THOUGHTS

_____

_____

_____

_____

_____

_____

_____

_____

_____

_____

_____

_____

_____

_____

_____

_____

_____

_____

It is in His divine will for us to possess gates and it is in our spiritual DNA to possess gates! If we can possess the gates, we can possess the city!

6

Don't Trade Your Mountain

Ultimately the devil wants to peddle his wares in exchange for our mountain of destiny. He wants everyone's destiny. He wants every high place, every lofty place and every mountain. He is greedy for elevated position. Let's once again look at the key Scripture for this book.

> "You were in Eden, the garden of God;
> Every precious stone was your covering:
> The ruby, the topaz and the diamond;
> The beryl, the onyx and the jasper;
> The lapis lazuli, the turquoise and the emerald;
> And the gold, the workmanship of your settings

and sockets, was in you.
On the day that you were created
They were prepared.
"You were the anointed cherub who covers,
And I placed you there.
You were on the holy mountain of God;
You walked in the midst of the stones of fire.
"You were blameless in your ways
From the day you were created
Until unrighteousness was found in you.
**"By the abundance of your trade
You were internally filled with violence,**
And you sinned;
**Therefore I have cast you as profane
From the mountain of God.**
And I have destroyed you, O covering cherub,
From the midst of the stones of fire.
"Your heart was lifted up because of your beauty;
You corrupted your wisdom by reason of your
splendor. **I cast you to the ground..."**
—Ezekiel 28:13-17

High Places

Originally Lucifer was on the holy mountain of God, but because he became filled with violence through an abundance of unrighteous trade, he was cast down from God's holy mountain. He was not content with the position that God gave to him. He was greedy for a more elevated position. He wanted to be in as elevated a position as the Creator God Himself. This greed for position cost him everything and he was cast down.

"How you have fallen from heaven,
O star of the morning, son of the dawn!
You have been cut down to the earth,
You who have weakened the nations!
"But you said in your heart,

'I will ascend to heaven;
I will raise my throne above the stars of God,
And I will sit on the mount of assembly
In the recesses of the north.
'I will ascend above the heights of the clouds;
I will make myself like the Most High.'"

—Isaiah 14:12-14

We know from Old Testament Scripture that the devil wanted all the "high places." High places are where he loves to be worshiped because he wants to be like God. He is still after the high places, our mountains of worship and destiny.

The enemy always uses deception, which is the stock and trade of the Kingdom of Darkness, because when we sin we actually unknowingly worship him, and that place of sin becomes a demonic Trading Floor (altar). Be not deceived, the enemy prowls around looking for someone who will trade his mountain in exchange for empty promises and faulty merchandise! He wants us to be cast down from our holy place in God into a place of sin, just like he was, because he is greedy and jealous for our position in God. A part of Satan's continuing ambition to replace God is his passionate yearnings to have others worship him. He is desperate for our worship! The place of prominence that he once enjoyed as a worshiper before the very throne of God has been lost for all eternity. That place of worship that was once Lucifer's has been transferred to us. As a result, he is out to sabotage our worship to God in an attempt to get the worship for himself.

No New Tricks

The enemy does not have any new tricks in his old black bag. He still uses the same devices on us that he used in the dispensation of the Old Testament and even attempted to use on Jesus Christ, the Son of the Living God. He mainly uses the deception of human appetite: lust of the flesh, lust of the eyes and the pride of life. In this chapter you will see, once again, how important it is to protect our spiritual gates.

> Do not love the world nor the things in the world. If anyone loves the world, the love of the Father is not in him. **For all that is in the world, the lust of the flesh and the lust of the eyes and the boastful pride of life, is not from the Father,** but is from the world. The world is passing away, and also its lusts; but the one who does the will of God lives forever.
>
> —1 John 2:15-17

Satan even had the audacity to tempt Jesus to worship him with hopes of Jesus trading His mountain of destiny as Messiah, the Savior of the world. Satan offered Jesus three trade schemes, but Jesus overcame every one of them with the Word of God. He overcame with Himself, because He is the Word of God. We still overcome the enemy with Jesus, the word of our testimony and the blood of the Lamb!

Lust of the Flesh

> Then Jesus was led up by the Spirit into the wilderness to be tempted by the devil. And after He had fasted forty days and forty nights, He then became hungry. And the tempter came and said to Him, **"If You are the Son of God, command that these stones become bread." But He answered and said, "It is written, 'MAN SHALL NOT LIVE ON BREAD ALONE, BUT ON EVERY WORD THAT PROCEEDS OUT OF THE MOUTH OF GOD.'"**
>
> —Matthew 4:1-4

The enemy tried to tempt Jesus to create food outside of the will of God. He thought he could get Jesus to fall for that scheme, because Jesus had just gone forty days without food and He was hungry. The desire for food is powerful because it is an innate desire within mankind. The enemy will capitalize on it in our weakest moments, if he can.

After all, it worked on Adam and Eve. They traded dominion of the earth for a piece of fruit. Do you think they really thought tasting one piece of forbidden fruit would cost them their dominion over the earth? Their entire inheritance in God was lost in trade for one piece of forbidden fruit.

Esau traded his entire birthright for a bowl of lentil stew and bread!

> Isaac prayed to the LORD on behalf of his wife, because she was barren; and the LORD answered him and Rebekah his wife conceived. But the children struggled together within her; and she said, "If it is so, why then am I this way?" So she went to inquire of the LORD. The LORD said to her, "Two nations are in your womb; And two peoples will be separated from your body; And one people shall be stronger than the other; **And the older shall serve the younger."**

> When the boys grew up, Esau became a skillful hunter, a man of the field, but Jacob was a peaceful man, living in tents. Now Isaac loved Esau, because he had a taste for game, but Rebekah loved Jacob. When Jacob had cooked stew, Esau came in from the field and he was famished; and Esau said to Jacob, "Please let me have a swallow of that red stuff there, for I am famished." Therefore his name was called Edom. But Jacob said, "First sell me your birthright." Esau said, "Behold, I am about to die; so of what use then is the birthright to me?" **And Jacob said, "First swear to me"; so he swore to him, and sold his birthright to Jacob.**

Then Jacob gave Esau bread and lentil stew; and he ate and drank, and rose and went on his way. Thus Esau despised his birthright.
—Genesis 25:21-23, 27-34

Esau traded at his mouth gate after the smell of the stew first went in through his nose gate and the sight of it went through his eye gates.

The first thing we notice is that once Esau made the trade he began to despise his birthright, which was his mountain of destiny. Esau's mountain of destiny was as the firstborn son of Isaac. He was to become a great nation before God. Jacob was also to become a great nation before God but his destiny was not the destiny of the firstborn, as that legally belonged to Esau since he was born first. If Jacob was supposed to have the blessing of the firstborn then he would have been born first! That would have been very easy for God to manage, but God had something even greater for Jacob. Jacob traded his supernatural blessing as the child of promise, the promised Israel, for Esau's natural blessing, the blessing of the firstborn child.

We all know the story. When it was time to release the blessing of the firstborn, Jacob's mother Rebekah persuaded him to deceive his father Isaac into thinking he was Esau. Not only did Esau trade, but Rebekah and Jacob traded, as well, by using Sin's Intellectual Properties called lying and deception. God will never require us to use sin to accomplish His purposes! Sin is always the wrong answer!

Rebekah traded her family that day because she was narrow-minded and thought only the firstborn child could be blessed. From that moment on Esau not only despised his birthright but he despised his brother Jacob, as well. Immense contention and turmoil are now in Rebekah's home, so much so, that she has to send her beloved Jacob off to her brother Laban's house which is far, far away. We don't know if she ever saw her son again! Esau lost his birthright over a pot of stew. Rebekah lost her family and Jacob is running for his life.

Jacob traded his supernatural blessing for the natural blessing of his brother Esau when he told his father, "I am Esau." He received the blessing of Esau, but a curse was attached to it because he used lying and deception to receive it. Jacob did not have to lie to receive his blessing, because it was already with him in his mother's womb. The Lord's blessing was already there. God told Rebekah while Jacob was still in her womb. God is not limited to the blessing of the firstborn. Joseph was the eleventh of twelve sons, yet he had the double portion blessing of favor upon him. King David was the youngest of the sons of Jesse and had the blessing of the king of Israel upon him.

Jacob is sent away from the family he loves because his brother Esau wants to kill him. He goes to his Uncle Laban's house and ends up being deceived and cheated by his uncle in a land that is far away from home. Jacob agreed to work for seven years to receive his Uncle Laban's daughter Rachel as his wife, but after the seven years of labor were over Laban gave him his daughter Leah instead! When he woke up in the morning expecting to see Rachel, he saw Leah! When he confronted his Uncle Laban, he said, "It is not the practice in our place to marry off the younger before the firstborn." So there you have it. Jacob got the blessing of the firstborn, Leah! He made that trade many years before when his father, expecting to give the blessing to Esau, the firstborn, was deceived into pronouncing the blessing on Jacob instead! Now Jacob had to work for another seven years, a total of fourteen years to marry Rachel. Can you imagine how difficult it must have been for Jacob, who is now at least forty-seven years old or possibly much older, to work another seven years for Rachel after already working hard for seven years to earn her hand in marriage? Beware, lest your trade find you out!

The Trading Floors

Eventually, Jacob wrestles with God and God deals with his sin nature. Jacob receives the blessing of becoming the promised Israel. But just think how different his life would have been if he had never traded his birthright for Esau's in the first place!

(You can read the whole story of Jacob in the book of Genesis beginning with Chapter 25.)

Lust of the Eyes

Again, the devil took Him to a very high mountain and showed Him all the kingdoms of the world and their glory; and he said to Him, "All these things I will give You, if You fall down and worship me." Then Jesus said to him, **"Go, Satan! For it is written, 'YOU SHALL WORSHIP THE LORD YOUR GOD, AND SERVE HIM ONLY.'"**
—Matthew 4:8-10

Lust of the eyes is another scheme that the enemy will use to tempt us to trade our mountain of destiny.

Satan tried to get Jesus to look with His eyes at all the glory He could possess, if He would just worship him. Jesus knew that the kingdoms of this world would become the kingdoms of our God and His Christ, so that was a lame idea on the devil's part. I guess we can't blame him for trying. The devil was fearful of Jesus and was desperate to make a trade to stop Him. The devil is afraid of you because you have Jesus, the hope of glory, within you. You have the same Spirit that raised Jesus Christ from the dead in you and greater is He who is in you than he who is in the world. You are a threat to the Kingdom of Darkness just as Jesus was a threat. Even though we are a threat to the dark kingdom, Jesus is able to keep us from stumbling in demonic trades!

Now to Him who is able to keep you from stumbling, and to make you stand in the

100

presence of His glory blameless with great joy.
—Jude 1:24

We need to become consciously aware of where our eyes are drawn. We also need to make a covenant with our eyes by consecrating them to God.

"I have made a covenant with my eyes; how then could I gaze at a virgin?"
—Job 31:1

One biblical character who stumbled in the area of lust of the eyes was Samson. Samson had a weakness and the enemy knew it. His weakness was with women "who looked good." Samson did not learn to consecrate his eye gates and it cost him greatly on the Trading Floors!

Then Samson went down to Timnah and saw a woman in Timnah, one of the daughters of the Philistines. So he came back and told his father and mother, "I saw a woman in Timnah, one of the daughters of the Philistines; now therefore, get her for me as a wife." Then his father and his mother said to him, "Is there no woman among the daughters of your relatives, or among all our people, that you go to take a wife from the uncircumcised Philistines?" But Samson said to his father, **"Get her for me, for she looks good to me."** However, his father and mother did not know that it was of the Lord, for He was seeking an occasion against the Philistines. Now at that time the Philistines were ruling over Israel.

Then Samson went down to Timnah with his father and mother, and came as far as the vineyards of Timnah; and behold, a young lion came roaring toward him. The Spirit of the Lord

came upon him mightily, so that he tore him as one tears a young goat though he had nothing in his hand; but he did not tell his father or mother what he had done. **So he went down and talked to the woman; and she looked good to Samson.**
—Judges 14:1-7

This Scripture makes it very clear that it was all about looks for Samson. It was all about the eye gates and what looked good to his eyes. Samson wanted what he saw. He did not heed his parents' instruction to take a wife from his own relatives. This was just the first woman that Samson saw and wanted; eventually, he saw Delilah and wanted her.

Samson was so overcome with lust for Delilah that he ultimately became blindsided and lost his ministry of supernatural strength, power and glory. Lust of the eyes blinded him, so much so, that he lost all common sense and told Delilah the secret to his supernatural strength, which was consecration to the Lord through a Nazarite vow.

In case you are not familiar with the story, you may want to read Judges 13-16. The secret to Samson's strength was the fact that he was born a Nazarite. His hair had never been cut in obedience to the Nazarite vow. Delilah deceived Samson and cut his hair while he slept with his head on her lap. He was then overtaken by the Philistines because all his strength was gone. The Philistines blinded him in both eyes, which is of great significance. The Philistines could have done a number of things to Samson but they chose to take his eyesight away. His eyesight, the very thing that Satan used to tempt him, became the price tag of the trade; and Samson became a slave to the Philistines for the rest of his life.

...for by what a man is overcome, by this he is enslaved.
—2 Peter 2:19

Samson was overcome by lust of the eyes and it caused him to become a blinded slave of the Philistines. That is a natural picture of what happens in the spirit realm when we trade at the gates. We become totally powerless and our mountain of destiny is open for trade with the gates of hell. Satan was after Samson's mountain which was supernatural strength to conquer and destroy the enemies of God. He had just come down "his mountain of destiny" as a deliverer of the nation of Israel when he saw a woman.

> When it was told to the Gazites, saying, "Samson has come here," **they surrounded the place and lay in wait for him all night at the gate of the city.** And they kept silent all night, saying, "Let us wait until the morning light, then we will kill him." Now Samson lay until midnight, and at midnight **he arose and took hold of the doors of the city gate and the two posts and pulled them up along with the bars; then he put them on his shoulders and carried them up to the top of the mountain which is opposite Hebron.**
>
> **After this it came about that he loved a woman in the valley of Sorek, whose name was Delilah. The lords of the Philistines came up to her and said to her, "Entice him, and see where his great strengths lies and how we may over power him that we may bind him to afflict him.** Then we will each give you eleven hundred pieces of silver."
>
> —Judges 16:2-5

Samson was on top of his mountain of destiny in God. He had just possessed the gates of his enemies and the enemy was desperate to make a trade. The enemy is SURE to try to make a trade right before or right after a great victory. The Scripture says that he loved a woman in the valley of Sorek. One of the meanings of the word *love* in this verse is human appetite for objects such as food, drink, sleep, etc. He had an uncontrollable appetite for what he saw and it cost him greatly on the Trading Floors.

Samson waited a bit too long to call on the Lord for help in the time of temptation. He eventually did call on the Lord and he killed more Philistines in his death than in his life. God is so merciful and such an amazing Redeemer! He is always there for us. He will never leave us nor forsake us, and nothing can separate us from His great love!

Here is how Samson's story ends:

> **Then Samson called to the LORD and said, "O Lord GOD, please remember me and please strengthen me just this time, O God, that I may at once be avenged of the Philistines for my two eyes."** Samson grasped the two middle pillars on which the house rested, and braced himself against them, the one with his right hand and the other with his left. And Samson said, "Let me die with the Philistines!" And he bent with all his might so that the house fell on the lords and all the people who were in it. **So the dead whom he killed at his death were more than those whom he killed in his life.** Then his brothers and all his father's household came down, took him, brought him up and buried him between Zorah and Eshtaol in the tomb of Manoah his father. Thus he had judged Israel twenty years.
>
> —Judges 16:28-31

Even when we mess up and make a wrong trade God is faithful to wipe away our transgression. He will never remember our sin, as was the case with Samson.

> **"I, even I, am the one who wipes out your transgressions for My own sake, and I will not remember your sins."**
>
> —Isaiah 43:25

Samson is listed in the great hall of fame in Hebrews 11. God sees past our weakness and sees our greatness. Only He can do that because He is God. There is none like Him!

> And what more shall I say? For time will fail
> me if I tell of Gideon, Barak, Samson, Jephthah,
> of David and Samuel and the prophets, who by
> faith conquered kingdoms, performed acts of
> righteousness, obtained promises, shut the mouths
> of lions, quenched the power of fire, escaped the
> edge of the sword, from weakness were made
> strong, became mighty in war, put foreign armies
> to flight.
> —Hebrews 11:32-34

Even though Samson made a disastrous trade on the Trading Floors, in the end when he repented and honored God, then God honored him. Samson's life ended in amazing triumph for the Kingdom of God and he goes down in history as a great hero of faith! There is just no one like our great God!

The Pride of Life

> Then the devil took Him into the holy city and
> had Him stand on the pinnacle of the temple, and
> said to Him, **"If You are the Son of God, throw
> Yourself down;** for it is written, 'He will command
> His angels concerning You'; and 'On their hands
> they will bear You up, So that You will not strike
> Your foot against a stone.'" **Jesus said to him, "On
> the other hand, it is written, 'You shall not put
> the Lord your God to the test.'"**
> —Matthew 4:5-7

The devil tried to tempt Jesus to show off as the Son of God. Pride always wants to make a show for other people. The unfortunate thing is that when we perform for man we get man's blessing, not the Lord's blessing. One biblical character that exemplifies this is King Saul. Time and again he demonstrated his desire for the approval of the people over the approval of God. If you study Saul's life, you will see that he was always more interested in building his own kingdom than God's Kingdom.

One of the first mistakes Saul made as the king of Israel was taking it upon himself to offer the burnt offering and the peace offerings in preparation for battle with the Philistines. He was instructed to wait for the Prophet Samuel to perform the sacrifices. Kings were not supposed to offer sacrifices to the Lord because that was solely the duty of the priests and prophets. Saul was more concerned about the people who were watching than he was in obeying God, who was also watching.

> **But Samuel said, "What have you done?" And
> Saul said, "Because I saw that the people were
> scattering from me,** and that you did not come
> within the appointed days, and that the Philistines
> were assembling at Michmash, therefore I said,
> 'Now the Philistines will come down against me at
> Gilgal, and I have not asked the favor of the LORD.'
> So I forced myself and offered the burnt offering."
> —1 Samuel 13:11-12

Saul was afraid of the people leaving him more than he was afraid of God leaving him. He cared more about what people thought than what God thought. The devil used the pride of life to steal his mountain of destiny as the king of Israel. That one trade of pride (thinking he was holy enough to perform the offerings before the Lord) cost him his destiny as the king of Israel!

> **Samuel said to Saul, "You have acted foolishly;
> you have not kept the commandment of the
> LORD your God, which He commanded you,**

**for now the LORD would have established your
kingdom over Israel forever. But now your
kingdom shall not endure.**

—1 Samuel 13:13

Saul's kingdom would have been established in Israel forever, but because of the sin of pride he lost it! He lost his mountain of destiny forever.

The one thing the Lord requires of us is to be humble. He gives grace to the humble but opposes the proud.

**He has told you, O man, what is good;
And what does the LORD require of you
But to do justice, to love kindness,
And to walk humbly with your God?**

—Micah 6:8

The Lord doesn't require very much from us. He is actually very easy to please, because Jesus already fulfilled every requirement necessary for us to have favor with God. Jesus gave us His right standing with God and all we have to do is accept His righteousness as our own by faith.

What is required of us is to do justice, love kindness and walk humbly with our God. All the rest has been done for us by the perfect work of Jesus on the cross. Because Jesus climbed Mount Calvary we can climb our mountain of destiny. He will keep us blameless until the day of His coming! Jesus' destiny was to die on a mountain so that we could climb ours, and accomplish all that He originally planned and purposed for us to do from the foundation of the world.

The story of King Saul does not have a redemptive ending like most other Bible stories because he continued to disobey God for the sake of the people. You can read the full account of Saul's life in 1 Samuel 9-31.

Merciful High Priest

But there is good news for us because our great High Priest, the Lord Jesus Christ, is compassionate and merciful. He was tempted in every way just like we are, yet He was without sin and He is able to come to our aid every time we are tempted!

> **Therefore, He had to be made like His brethren in all things, so that He might become a merciful and faithful high priest in things pertaining to God, to make propitiation for the sins of the people. For since He Himself was tempted in that which He has suffered, He is able to come to the aid of those who are tempted.**
> —Hebrews 2:17-18

No matter what temptation we may face, He is there and has already overcome it for us. We just need to call His Name!

> "These things I have spoken to you, so that in Me you may have peace. **In the world you have tribulation, but take courage; I have overcome the world.**"
> —John 16:33

He has overcome the world, so you can overcome the world through Him! You can take your mountain! See you at the top!

LIFE APPLICATION SECTION

Memory Verse:

Do not love the world nor the things in the world. If anyone loves the world, the love of the Father is not in him. For all that is in the world, the lust of the flesh and the lust of the eyes and the boastful pride of life, is not from the Father, but is from the world. The world is passing away, and also its lusts; but the one who does the will of God lives forever.

—1 John 2:15-17

Reflections:

How did Esau, Rachel and Jacob trade?

_____

_____

_____

How did Samson trade?

_____

_____

_____

How did Saul trade?

_____

_____

_____

The Trading Floors

JOURNAL YOUR THOUGHTS

_____

_____

_____

_____

_____

_____

_____

_____

_____

_____

_____

_____

_____

_____

_____

_____

_____

_____

_____

The enemy always uses deception, the stock and trade of the Kingdom of Darkness, because when we sin we actually unknowingly worship him, and that place of sin becomes a demonic Trading Floor.

THE THRESHING FLOOR
PATHWAY TO GLORY

The purpose of this chapter, as well as the next regarding threshing floors, is to illustrate the power of sacrifice, because in essence a threshing floor is a Trading Floor in the realm of the spirit.

We have been told by the prophetic voices of the Church that this year of 2014 is the "Year of the Open Door." Many of us are at the threshold of destiny after many long years of preparation. As the Church, we are on the threshold of the next "Great Awakening" and the biggest harvest of souls the Church has ever seen. We know there will be more revivalists in this next move of God than any other move of God in the history of mankind. It is going to take all hands on deck to bring in this great "end-time" harvest of souls. God is looking for more Peters, James and Johns in our day. He is looking for those who will place everything they have on His Trading Floor called "the altar," to become the greatest fishers of men the world has ever seen. Yes, the best for the age of the Church is still to come. The Lord is saving the best for last. Those who are last will be first and the first will be last! Many of God's people have been in preparation for this great outpouring of God's Spirit for many years, some decades. Every great move of God was preceded by several great men and women who would pay the price on the threshing floor. One very influential national prophet titled this year, "See Your Pathway to the Open Door." The pathway is the way to the threshing floor. It precedes and is at the threshold of the open door to destiny!

> "So rejoice, O sons of Zion,
> And be glad in the Lord your God;
> For He has given you the early rain
> for your vindication.
> And He has poured down for you the rain,
> The early and latter rain as before.
> **The threshing floors will be full of grain,**
> **And the vats will overflow with the**
> **new wine and oil.**
> **"It will come about after this**
> That I will pour out My Spirit on all mankind;
> And your sons and daughters will prophesy,
> Your old men will dream dreams,
> Your young men will see visions.
> "Even on the male and female servants
> I will pour out My Spirit in those days."
> —Joel 2:23-24, 28-29

The Overflow

"The threshing floors will be full of grain,
And the vats will overflow with the new wine
and oil."

—Joel 2:24

There are many types and symbols throughout the word of God. Grain or wheat symbolizes the "product of the Holy Spirit." The product of the Holy Spirit is proven godly character. The wheat, new wine and oil are many times mentioned together in Scripture, and almost always the wheat is mentioned first. God is very intentional in everything that He says and does. The wheat is mentioned first because that is the order of first things. We have to have wheat, "the product of the Holy Spirit," which is proven godly character, before we will be eligible for the new wine, which symbolizes the "fullness of the Holy Spirit." We must have the wheat, "the product of the Holy Spirit," and the new wine, "the fullness of the Holy Spirit," before we will be eligible to receive the oil, "the power of the Holy Spirit." The Scripture tells us that in the last days the threshing floors will be full of grain, and the vats will overflow with new wine and oil. According to this Scripture in Joel, the overflow of wheat, wine and oil precede a move of God's Spirit. This is where we are right now as the Church of the Lord Jesus Christ. God is checking the threshing floors and vats for the overflow of His Spirit in our lives.

Threshing Floor

So what is a threshing floor? In biblical days after the harvest, the grain was placed on a flat surface, which was hard and smooth. This place was known as the threshing floor. The process of threshing was performed generally by spreading the sheaves of wheat across the hard threshing floor. Sometimes the wheat was beaten manually and other times oxen and cattle were used to tread over the grain repeatedly, which loosened the edible part of wheat grain from the scaly, inedible hard chaff that surrounded it. The threshing floor was usually in a high place so the chaff could be caught by the wind. Winnowing forks were used to throw the wheat mixture into the air so the wind could blow away the chaff, leaving only the product of good grain on the floor.[1]

Now let us look at verse 28:

"It will come about after this
That I will pour out My Spirit on all mankind;
And your sons and daughters will prophesy,
Your old men will dream dreams,
Your young men will see visions."
—Joel 2:28

We are all familiar with this verse which promises the great outpouring of God's Spirit for all mankind. As a matter of fact in Acts 2, Peter recites this passage of Scripture on the day of Pentecost, the first great outpouring of the Holy Spirit.

Shortly after Peter proclaimed this, 3,000 souls were saved and the Scripture says that great signs and wonders were taking place through the apostles. The acts of the apostles are what we long to happen again in our day. The beginning of Joel 2:28 says, *"after this"* – after what? After the threshing floors are full of wheat and the vats of new wine and oil overflow (2:24). That is the timing of when the great outpouring of His Spirit will be released.

In order to pass through the threshold of the open door to personal revival and fulfilled destiny, we will have to embrace the threshing floor. Remember, before this powerful ministry was demonstrated through Peter, Jesus told him that he would be "sifted" like wheat.

"Simon, Simon, behold, Satan has demanded
permission **to sift you like wheat;** but I have
prayed for you, that your faith may not fail; and
you, when once you have turned again, strengthen
your brothers."
—Luke 22:31-32

Peter embraced this sifting through deep repentance after denying the Lord on the night He was betrayed. The product of the Holy Spirit, proven godly character, became evident in Peter's life. He strengthened his brothers on the day of Pentecost and throughout his life, and was also the first apostolic evangelist to arise in his day. Peter could have stayed in self-pity and shame, but instead, he chose God's pathway of repentance.

The threshing floor is where God develops His character in us. It can be found on the pathway to the open door of glory that awaits us. Many of the trades that bring the greatest return happen on the threshing floor when we embrace the pathway of being "sifted" or "treaded upon" like wheat, just like Peter did.

Trading Death for Life

> And Jesus answered them, saying, "The hour has come for the Son of Man to be glorified. **Truly, truly, I say to you, unless a grain of wheat falls into the earth and dies, it remains alone; but if it dies, it bears much fruit.** He who loves his life loses it, and he who hates his life in this world will keep it to life eternal."
>
> —John 12:23-25

Jesus likens His own body to a grain of wheat that had to fall to the ground and die in order for the harvest of salvation for the world to come.

Paul understood the concept of trading death for life. If we want to save our lives, we must lose them. To the measure we embrace death to self is the same measure that we will embrace the power of His resurrection.

> And may be found in Him, not having a righteousness of my own derived from the Law, but that which is through faith in Christ, the righteousness which comes from God on the basis of faith, **that I may know Him and the power of His resurrection and the fellowship of His**

sufferings, being conformed to His death; in order that I may attain to the resurrection from the dead.
—Philippians 3:9-11

Then Jesus said to His disciples, "If anyone wishes to come after Me, he must deny himself, and take up his cross and follow Me. For whoever wishes to save his life will lose it; **but whoever loses his life for My sake will find it.**"
—Matthew 16:24-25

Right here, God is offering us a trade on the Trading Floor of Heaven: Our life and what we have planned for ourselves while on earth, for His life and what He planned for us from the foundation of the world. Many times His plans include the threshing floor, the wine press and the oil presses of life. His goal is to produce the product, fullness and power of the Holy Spirit in our lives. The outcome of glory comes with a price for those who are willing to trade on the Trading Floor with God! Jesus said narrow is the way to life and only a few find it. Only a few are willing to choose this narrow way of pressure for glory. Many are called but few are chosen. Those who embrace this narrow way will eventually be the ones chosen for His glory!

Ruth's Trade

One person who willingly traded pressure for glory was Naomi's daughter-in-law, Ruth. Ruth chose a narrow path by following Naomi back to Bethlehem. Ruth left her family, hometown, and everything that was safe and familiar to her to follow Naomi to an unfamiliar land.

But Ruth said, "Do not urge me to leave you or turn back from following you; for where you go, I will go, and where you lodge, I will lodge. Your people shall be my people, and your God, my God. **Where you die, I will die, and there I will be**

buried. Thus may the Lord do to me, and worse, if anything but death parts you and me."
—Ruth 1:16-17

Ruth was willing to lay her own life down to remain loyal to and care for her mother-in-law Naomi. She was selfless in her love towards Naomi. Ruth was young and could have chosen to abide in her own hometown with her own people to find another husband, just like Naomi's other daughter-in-law, Orpah, chose to do. There was something very unique about Ruth. It is called selflessness.

Ruth also possessed a spirit of humility. She honored Naomi by obeying everything Naomi told her to do, which included a trip to the threshing floor at night in her best dress to lay at the feet of a strange man!

> Then Naomi her mother-in-law said to her, "My daughter, shall I not seek security for you that it may be well with you? Now is not Boaz our kinsman, with whose maids you were? **Behold, he winnows barley at the threshing floor tonight. Wash yourself therefore, and anoint yourself and put on your best clothes, and go down to the threshing floor;** but do not make yourself known to the man until he has finished eating and drinking. It shall be when he lies down, that you shall notice the place where he lies, and you shall go and uncover his feet and lie down; then he will tell you what you shall do." She said to her, **"All that you say I will do."**
> —Ruth 3:1-5

In humility Ruth obeys her mother-in-law and goes to the threshing floor washed, anointed and in her best clothes, and secretly lies down at the feet of Boaz.

Boaz means "kinsman, redeemer." Ruth is a picture of the Bride of Christ at the feet of Jesus in worship on the threshing floor, the place where self is denied and new life comes.

Ruth went to the threshing floor in secret, and Boaz marries her because of the time they shared together on the threshing floor.

> But you, when you pray, go into your inner
> room, close your door and pray to your Father
> who is in secret, **and your Father who sees
> what is done in secret will reward you.**
> —Matthew 6:6

In 2 Kings 4, this principle of secrecy with God is found in a story about a widow in Elisha's day. The creditors were going to take her two sons because she couldn't pay her bills. Elisha told her to take what she had in oil and begin to pour it into borrowed vessels. As she did this behind closed doors, where no one else could see what she was doing, the oil multiplied, she paid off her debts and was able to live on the rest of the income from the oil. The secret is pouring out what we have to the Lord behind closed doors where only He can see us.

Jesus tells us to pray in secret; if we pray to be noticed by men then we have our reward in full. The trade has been made; the reward is the accolades of men instead of the Father's reward.

Because Ruth chose humility and the pathway to the hard place called the threshing floor, she was redeemed from famine. Ruth became a landowner and one of the wealthiest women in Bethlehem, all because she was humble and chose to embrace the threshing floor. What a difficult and humbling experience for Ruth to get all dressed up just to go lie on a dirty threshing floor at some man's feet in the middle of the night! But that one trade of obedience and humility brought a lifetime of reward to Ruth. She became not only the wealthy wife of a landowner, but she also became a mother, a grandmother and the great-grandmother of King David, the greatest worshiper who ever lived. Ruth the Moabitess is now mentioned in the lineage of Jesus Christ the Messiah. The trade of humility and obedience on the threshing floor brought the Seed of Glory that would change the history of the entire world.

When we choose the threshing floor the Lord will redeem us from every kind of spiritual famine, and as we will see in the next chapter, financial famine as well.

From a Distance

In Genesis 22 when Abraham was preparing to sacrifice Isaac to the Lord, the Scripture says, *"On the third day Abraham raised his eyes and saw the place from a distance"* (verse 4). We are in the "Third Day of the Church" and many of us can see this place of sacrifice off in the distance, but we have not chosen to embrace it yet. To the measure we embrace sacrifice and death to self, is the same measure that we will experience resurrection and new life. In the Kingdom of God, self-sacrifice, even of our own hopes and dreams in the Lord, brings the highest dividends on the Trading Floor of Heaven.

One Thing You Still Lack

God is asking for some of us to "give up" and some of us "to take up" on the Trading Floor of Heaven. What do you need to give up or what do you need to take up in order to fulfill your destiny?

The rich young ruler was given the greatest opportunity of all: The chance to become one of Jesus' chosen disciples. But he wasn't willing to "give up" what God was asking of him. He did not want to make a trade of sacrifice for the glory of becoming one of Jesus' chosen disciples!

> A ruler questioned Him, saying, "Good Teacher, what shall I do to inherit eternal life?" And Jesus said to him, "Why do you call Me good? No one is good except God alone. You know the

commandments, 'Do not commit adultery, Do not murder, Do not steal, Do not bear false witness, Honor your father and mother.'" And he said, "All these things I have kept from my youth." When Jesus heard this, He said to him, **"One thing you still lack; sell all that you possess and distribute it to the poor, and you shall have treasure in heaven; and come, follow Me."** But when he had heard these things, he became very sad, for he was extremely rich.

—Luke 18:17-23

Right here and now, God is showing us each individually, that "one thing that we still lack" before we can cross the threshold into the door of our destiny. For some of us, destiny will require us to "take up" more time at the feet of Jesus, for others it will require us to "give up" something that is causing us to stumble. The rich young ruler, whose name we do not know, could have had his name go down in history with the rest of the disciples who chose to leave everything to follow Jesus. He was personally offered this chance while he was face-to-face with Jesus of Nazareth! He could have stored up masses of treasures in Heaven. Plus, according to the Bible, he would have received up to one hundred times what he gave up during His lifetime here on earth. However, he chose not to trade; he did not want to "give up" what the Lord was asking of him. How sad, we don't even know if he made it into Heaven. No one knows his name and he is never again mentioned in Scripture.

Prophetically, I sense that many of us have been sowing into our destinies for quite some time, and now the altars on the Trading Floor are ready to tip back to earth in our favor. We just need to add that "one thing that we still lack."

After many years of sowing in tears, God's Trading Floor is about to open and pour out in favor of destiny for His Church!

Paying Full Price

King David also knew the power of trading on a threshing floor. Let's visit the main passage of Scripture for this story:

> **…And the angel of the Lord stood by the
> threshing floor of Ornan the Jebusite.** Then
> David lifted up his eyes and saw the angel of the
> Lord standing between earth and heaven, with
> his drawn sword in his hand stretched out over
> Jerusalem. Then David and the elders, covered
> with sackcloth, fell on their faces. David said to
> God, "Is it not I who commanded to count the
> people? Indeed, I am the one who has sinned and
> done very wickedly, but these sheep, what have
> they done? O Lord my God, please let Your hand
> be against me and my father's household, but not
> against Your people that they should be plagued."
> **Then the angel of the Lord commanded Gad to
> say to David, that David should go up and build
> an altar to the Lord on the threshing floor of
> Ornan the Jebusite.**
> —1 Chronicles 21:15-18

The reason David found himself in trouble in the first place is because Satan moved him to number Israel, which is not something a king was to do unless directed by God. If Israel was numbered, a ransom was to be offered to the Lord for each soul. This one trade of prideful disobedience angered the Lord to the point that He was going to destroy Jerusalem, the City of David. But David and the elders repented and the Lord gave David a means of trade to make it right before Him. The trade would be sacrifice on a threshing floor that David would purchase for full price.

> Then David said to Ornan, "Give me the site of
> this threshing floor that I may build on it an altar

to the Lord; for the full price you shall give it to me, that the plague may be restrained from the people." Ornan said to David, "Take it for yourself; and let my lord the king do what is good in his sight. See, I will give the oxen for burnt offerings and the threshing sledges for wood and the wheat for the grain offering; I will give it all." But King David said to Ornan, **"No, but I will surely buy it for the full price; for I will not take what is yours for the Lord, or offer a burnt offering which costs me nothing." So David gave Ornan 600 shekels of gold by weight for the site. Then David built an altar to the Lord there and offered burnt offerings and peace offerings. And he called to the Lord and He answered him with fire from heaven on the altar of burnt offering. The Lord commanded the angel, and he put his sword back in its sheath.**
—1 Chronicles 21:21-27

David made peace with God on a threshing floor. Note that he could have gotten this place for free, but he said, *"No, but I will surely buy it for the full price; for I will not take what is yours for the Lord, or offer a burnt offering which costs me nothing."* Then David built an altar, placed offerings on it and the Lord answered by fire on the threshing floor. The threshing floor is a very costly place. Sometimes it will cost us everything that we have to embrace the glory of fulfilled destiny. This was the beginning of fulfilled destiny for the House of David. David's deepest desire was to build a glorious house for the God of Israel, a place where the Presence of the Lord could comfortably dwell.

Then Solomon began to build the house of the Lord in **Jerusalem on Mount Moriah, where the Lord had appeared to his father David, at the**

**place that David had prepared on the threshing
floor of Ornan the Jebusite.**

—2 Chronicles 3:1

Place of Provision

Not only is this building site for the temple of Solomon the
threshing floor that David purchased for full price, but this is also
the place that Abraham saw in the distance on the third day as he
traveled to offer Isaac to the Lord. This became a place of God's
supernatural provision for destiny! Abraham saw a threshing floor
in the distance. He embraced obedience on the threshing floor, and
we find that the sacrifice of his son was not required. God provided
a ram in the thicket for him to sacrifice instead. This was a picture
of the sacrificial trade of the Lord Jesus Christ, the Lamb of God,
who takes away the sins of the world.

> Abraham called the name of that place The Lord
> Will Provide, as it is said to this day, **"In the
> mount of the Lord it will be provided."**
> —Genesis 22:14

When we embrace the threshing floor like Abraham and
David did, then the Lord brings supernatural provision for our
destiny. This place called *Jehovah Jireh* played a significant role in
the destiny of both Abraham and David.

For Abraham this was the place where he proved absolute
loyalty and obedience to the Lord. This one act of obedience was
the righteous trade that would tip the altars on Heaven's Trading
Floor in Abraham's favor.

> **Then the angel of the Lord called to Abraham a
> second time from heaven, and said, "By Myself
> I have sworn, declares the Lord, because you
> have done this thing and have not withheld your
> son,** your only son, indeed I will greatly bless you,

and I will greatly multiply your seed as the stars
of the heavens and as the sand which is on the
seashore; and your seed shall possess the gate of
their enemies. **In your seed all the nations of the
earth shall be blessed, because you have obeyed
My voice."**

—Genesis 22:15-18

Abraham had been sowing into his destiny to become the
"Father of Many Nations" from the first day he received the promise
in Genesis 12. He began to sacrifice to the Lord immediately. But
it would take this significant trade of obedience to tip the altars
in his favor. The Lord revealed to me the reason why Abraham
had to wait twenty-five years for the promise of Isaac — This long-
awaited promise caused Abraham's act of obedience to produce
exponentially more power on the Trading Floor. The technology
of sacrifice yields the highest dividends on the Trading Floors, and
the greater the sacrifice the greater the power. How much more
worth did Isaac have in Abraham's heart after having to wait for
him for twenty-five years? What would be the chances of Abraham
having another son, especially from Sarah, the love of his life?
What we sacrifice has to be in direct proportion to the promised
destiny. Abraham was being given the opportunity to be the
"Father of Many Nations," so he had to offer something to God in
direct proportion to the promise. But because God is so generous
and very wealthy, we always receive thirty, sixty or a hundredfold
more than we give on our side of the trade.

Many of us have been sowing just like Abraham. It may just
take one last act of obedience on the threshing floor to tip the altars
of Heaven in our favor!

Glory Manifests on the Threshing Floor

Mount Moriah would one day become the threshing floor of
Ornan and would be purchased by King David. The site of this
threshing floor would one day become the building site of King

Solomon's temple, the most glorious temple ever built in the history of mankind. Kings and queens from around the world would come to visit this glorious place laden with gifts for the king of Israel, but even more significant is the fact that this is the very place where the glory became so thick that the priests could not even stand to minister!

> When the priests came forth from the holy place (for all the priests who were present had sanctified themselves, without regard to divisions), and all the Levitical singers, Asaph, Heman, Jeduthun, and their sons and kinsmen, clothed in fine linen, with cymbals, harps and lyres, standing east of the altar, and with them one hundred and twenty priests blowing trumpets in unison when the trumpeters and the singers were to make themselves heard with one voice to praise and to glorify the Lord, and when they lifted up their voice accompanied by trumpets and cymbals and instruments of music, and when they praised the Lord saying, "He indeed is good for His lovingkindness is everlasting," **then the house, the house of the Lord, was filled with a cloud, so that the priests could not stand to minister because of the cloud, for the glory of the Lord filled the house of God.**
>
> —2 Chronicles 5:11-14

The house of the Lord was built on a threshing floor and it was filled with GLORY! There were 120 priests blowing the trumpets the day the glory came to Solomon's temple, which is very significant, because there were 120 priests of God (believers) in the upper room when the Glory came the first time in the New Covenant Church.

> At this time Peter stood up in the midst of the brethren **(a gathering of about one hundred and**

twenty persons was there together).

—Acts 1:15

When the day of Pentecost had come, they were all together in one place. And suddenly there came from heaven a noise like a violent rushing wind, **and it filled the whole house where they were sitting.**

—Acts 2:1-2

But Peter, standing up with the eleven, raised his voice and said to them, "Men of Judea and all who dwell in Jerusalem, let this be known to you, and heed my words. For these are not drunk, as you suppose, since it is only the third hour of the day. But this is what was spoken by the prophet Joel:
'And it shall come to pass
in the last days, says God,
That I will pour out of My Spirit on all flesh;
Your sons and your daughters shall prophesy,
Your young men shall see visions,
Your old men shall dream dreams.
And on My menservants and on
My maidservants
I will pour out My Spirit in those days;
And they shall prophesy.
I will show wonders in heaven above
And signs in the earth beneath:
Blood and fire and vapor of smoke.
The sun shall be turned into darkness,
And the moon into blood,
Before the coming of the great
and awesome day of the Lord.
And it shall come to pass
That whoever calls on the name of the Lord
Shall be saved."'

—Acts 2:14-21 NKJV

All the tears that have been shed on the hard threshing floors of life by God's faithful men and women are about to tip back to earth. We are going to experience the rain of God like we've never experienced before. Those who have sown in tears are going to reap the harvest and everlasting joy will be theirs!

Glory Birthed on the Threshing Floor

The Glory of God is Jesus Christ. Jesus Christ in us, the hope of glory is about to be birthed at this place called the *threshing floor*.

Not only does the Messiah come through Ruth's lineage, but the place where her redemption occurred through her marriage covenant with Boaz, was the same place that the Messiah, the Lord Jesus Christ would be born, right there in Bethlehem of Judea! Jewish history tells us that the same place where Ruth met Boaz on the threshing floor is where Mary gave birth to Jesus our Messiah. It was called the "Shepherd's Field"!

The Bride of Christ who has embraced the threshing floor is about to birth the glorious second coming of the Lord Jesus Christ!

LIFE APPLICATION SECTION

Memory Verse:

And Jesus answered them, saying, "The hour has come for the Son of Man to be glorified. Truly, truly, I say to you, unless a grain of wheat falls into the earth and dies, it remains alone; but if it dies, it bears much fruit. He who loves his life loses it, and he who hates his life in this world will keep it to life eternal."

—John 12:23-25

Reflections:

What precedes the outpouring of God's Spirit according to Joel 2?

_____

_____

_____

What is at the threshold of the open door to destiny?

_____

_____

_____

What building site did God choose for Solomon's temple?

_____

_____

_____

JOURNAL YOUR THOUGHTS

_____

_____

_____

_____

_____

_____

_____

_____

_____

_____

_____

_____

_____

_____

_____

_____

_____

_____

_____

_____

_____

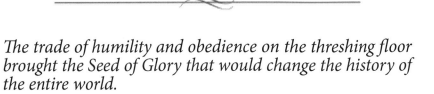

The trade of humility and obedience on the threshing floor brought the Seed of Glory that would change the history of the entire world.

THE THRESHING FLOOR – PATHWAY TO FINANCIAL BLESSING

Wealth attracts wealth and brings great influence. We can see how important it is for the expansion of God's Kingdom in the last days before Jesus' return. I believe God will release it to those of us who are prepared to righteously steward it. His path of preparation is probably not the pathway we would choose because His ways are higher and much different than ours.

One Saturday evening my pastor, Dr. Francis Myles, sent me a text message to ask if I would receive the offering for the next day's Sunday service. At that time, I had the priestly Order of Melchizedek, the threshing floor, camels and Isaiah 60 in my spirit. All four topics were floating around in my spirit at one time. I was sure the Lord wanted me to address one of them for the next day's offering. I had no idea He would ask me to address all four of them in one offering message. That seemed like quite a challenge, but at His direction I proceeded to search out the Scriptures and was amazed at what the Lord showed me. Once again, trading on the threshing floor is the pathway to glory for those of us who will embrace it.

This place called the threshing floor is where many of us are right now because we are at the threshold of the open door to destiny. This is a challenging, uncomfortable place where we can literally feel the crushing and bruising of our flesh. If you can relate to this, then you are at the right place at the right time, because the threshing floor not only precedes personal glory but it also precedes financial blessing, as you will soon discover.

Wealth is God's plan for His covenant children of Abraham and the threshing floor is on the pathway to receiving the blessing of Abraham. Even Abraham himself received his inheritance on that which would become a threshing floor.

The Order of Melchizedek

If we are going to walk in financial blessing, then it is very important for us to first understand that we are not under the priestly Order of Levi, which is tied to the Law. We are under the priestly Order of Melchizedek, which is tied to grace.

> Although He was a Son, He learned obedience from the things which He suffered. And having been made perfect, He became to all those who obey Him the source of eternal salvation, being designated by God as a **high priest according to the order of Melchizedek.**
> —Hebrews 5:8-10

> This hope we have as an anchor of the soul, a hope both sure and steadfast and one which enters

within the veil, where **Jesus has entered as a forerunner for us, having become a high priest forever according to the order of Melchizedek.**
—Hebrews 6:19-20

The New Testament Church of the Lord Jesus Christ is under the Order of Melchizedek. The Order of Levi has become obsolete and is ready to disappear.

When He said, "A new covenant," **He has made the first obsolete.** But whatever is becoming obsolete and growing old is ready to disappear.
—Hebrews 8:13

Grace Not Law

It is imperative that we understand this because the Order of Levi comes from Mount Sinai, the "Mountain of Law," but the Order of Melchizedek comes from Mount Calvary, the "Mountain of Grace." Anytime we trade grace (the Tree of Life), for law (the Tree of the Knowledge of Good and Evil), we end up cursed just like Adam and Eve did in the Garden of Eden. The curse started at a tree called the Tree of the Knowledge of Good and Evil, that represented the law, and ended at a tree on a hill called Calvary, that represented the grace and truth found only in the Lord Jesus Christ.

Adam and Eve had no knowledge of Sin until they ate of the Tree of the Knowledge of Good and Evil.

Because by the works of the Law no flesh will be justified in His sight; **for through the Law comes the knowledge of Sin.**
—Romans 3:20

Sin is what began to master all who ate from the Tree of the Knowledge of Good and Evil in the Garden of Eden. It was Sin that mastered Cain and caused him to kill his brother Abel.

**For sin shall not be master over you, for you are
not under law but under grace.**
—Romans 6:14

The Tree of Life represented the grace of the Lord Jesus Christ. Jesus set us free from the sin and death that comes through the Tree of Knowledge of Good and Evil.

For the law of the Spirit of life in Christ Jesus has
set you free from the law of sin and of death.
—Romans 8:2

Jesus became a curse so that the blessing of Abraham might come to us! That is why I am laying this important foundation of law versus grace, in order to explain how we can fully receive the blessing of Abraham.

Christ redeemed us from the curse of the Law,
having become a curse for us—for it is written,
"Cursed is everyone who hangs on a tree" —
**in order that in Christ Jesus the blessing of
Abraham might come to the Gentiles,** so that we
would receive the promise of the Spirit through
faith.
—Galatians 3:13-14

If we try to live our lives by our own righteous works of the Law, instead of by faith, we end up cursed, because not one of us can keep the whole Law. Only the Lord Jesus Christ was able to fulfill the Law and He did it all for us. The Scripture tells us that if we keep the whole Law but stumble at even one point of it we become guilty of all of it!

For whoever keeps the whole Law and **yet
stumbles in one point, he has become guilty
of all.**
—James 2:10

Many of today's ministers are still quoting from Malachi 3 when it comes to tithes and offerings and financial prosperity.

> "Will a man rob God? Yet you are robbing Me!
> But you say, 'How have we robbed You?' In tithes
> and offerings. **You are cursed with a curse**, for
> you are robbing Me, the whole nation of you!"
> —Malachi 3:8-9

The book of Malachi was written to the priesthood of Israel and the nation of Israel under the Law. But we, the Church of Jesus Christ, are not under the Law nor are we under the priesthood of Levi. Not all Scripture pertains to the dispensation of time that we live in today, especially regarding the Law of Moses.

God deals with us according to the revelation we have. If we are tithing with the fear of being cursed, in respect to the revelation in Malachi 3, then a curse could very well come upon us. For one thing, if we are tithing with this mentality then we need to keep the entire Law. For another, Job said that what he feared came upon him.

Many in the Body of Christ are living in financial bondage and I believe this is one of the reasons why: They have traded grace for law, the Order of Melchizedek for the Order of Levi.

The motivating factor behind this chapter is to see the fullness of the blessing of the gospel of Christ come upon the Church so that we can reap the end-time harvest of wealth and with it billions of lost souls.

As the Body of Christ we are entitled to the blessing of Abraham. If we are going to understand how to receive the blessing that our father Abraham walked in, we need to study his life.

> "Listen to me, you who pursue righteousness,
> Who seek the Lord:
> **Look to the rock from which you were hewn**
> **And to the quarry from which you were dug.**

"Look to Abraham your father
And to Sarah who gave birth to you in pain;
When he was but one I called him,
Then I blessed him and multiplied him."

—Isaiah 51:1-2

Honor and Holy Devotion, Not Fear

The very first thing Abraham did when he met King Melchizedek was offer Him a tenth of his spoil from the kingdoms he conquered in battle.

> For this Melchizedek, king of Salem, priest of the Most High God, who met Abraham as he was returning from the slaughter of the kings and blessed him, **to whom also Abraham apportioned a tenth part of all the spoils,** was first of all, by the translation of his name, king of righteousness, and then also king of Salem, which is king of peace.
>
> —Hebrews 7:1-2

When Abraham met Melchizedek in the Valley of Kings, Melchizedek blessed Abraham with the blessing of God Most High. This blessing radically changed Abraham's spiritual stature and standing in both Heaven and earth. Overwhelmed by this heavenly blessing, Abraham gave Melchizedek a tithe of honor. Consequently, Abraham was already blessed when he gave his tithes of honor! He did not tithe out of fear but out of honor and holy devotion.

> But the one whose genealogy is not traced from them collected a tenth from **Abraham and blessed the one who had the promises.**
>
> —Hebrews 7:6

Abraham was the first member of the Order of Melchizedek. The Lord said when he was but ONE He called him. The Order of Melchizedek is called an order because there is to be an "order of members." Melchizedek blessed Abraham, the one who already had the promises. Abraham would be the first of many to become part of this ancient eternal priestly order which holds the highest governmental rank in all of the earth (Daniel 2; Isaiah 9).

How many of us are the ones who already have the promises? We have the promises but we are waiting on the provision to fulfill them. One thing we must understand is that the blessing of Abraham flows from the eternal priestly Order of Melchizedek, not Levi. It flows from the "Mountain of Grace" not the "Mountain of Law."

Tithing is still for today. We are to tithe into the Order of Melchizedek, which is a tithe of love and honor, not obligation and fear. If we are to walk in the blessing of Abraham, we have to lay this very important foundation of grace in order to be rightly positioned to receive the blessing.

Why do we tithe? Because it is the way that God has chosen to bless us. Why would God choose tithing or giving as a way to bless us? We give because it is impossible to be greedy and generous at the same time. The love of money is the root of all kinds of evil. Giving destroys that root.

> "For where your treasure is, **there your heart will be also.**"
>
> —Luke 12:34

Ultimately, God wants our hearts, not our money. He knows if our treasure is in Heaven, then our hearts will be focused on Heaven as well.

There is so much more to be said regarding the Order of Melchizedek and tithing under the Order. I highly recommend that you read *Tithing Under the Order of Melchizedek: The Return of the Lost Key* by Dr. Francis Myles.

Abraham's Trade

Throughout history our father Abraham is known as a friend of God. Tithing is where Abraham started his friendship with God Most High, Possessor of Heaven and Earth. But much more would be required of Abraham if he were to become the father of many nations. If true multiplication was going to manifest, there would have to be death. Remember, unless a grain of wheat falls to the ground and dies it abides alone, but if it dies it will multiply and bear much fruit. Abraham was but one when God called him, but God multiplied him so that his descendants became like the sand on the seashore and the stars in the sky. Multiplication is our inheritance through the Abrahamic Covenant, which is an everlasting covenant. This covenant has even been made available to the Gentiles by the death of the Lord Jesus Christ.

> Now it came about after these things, **that God tested Abraham**, and said to him, "Abraham!" And he said, "Here I am." He said, "Take now your son, your only son, whom you love, Isaac, and go to the land of Moriah, and offer him there as a burnt offering on one of the mountains of which I will tell you." So Abraham rose early in the morning and saddled his donkey, and took two of his young men with him and Isaac his son; and he split wood for the burnt offering, and arose and went to the place of which God had told him. On the third day Abraham raised his eyes and saw the place from a distance.
>
> —Genesis 22:1-4

We see the absolute obedience and surrender of the father of our faith. He went to the place where God told him to go with every intention of offering Isaac, if it were required of him. Abraham was willing to sacrifice his only son by Sarah, their son of promise. Tithing may not have represented a very significant test for Abraham, as he was already very wealthy when he met Melchizedek in the Valley of Kings. Abraham could always create more wealth and accumulate more material possessions. But to ask for his son of promise, now that was a test of gigantic proportion! It took Abraham and Sarah twenty-five years to have Isaac, and he was their laughter, their son of promise. Another son at their age would be nearly impossible. Abraham knew it and God knew it.

Abraham was totally dead to himself and to his own will. The blessing was sure to follow, and it did. He is still known today as the Father of the Jewish Nation (sand on the seashore) and the Church (stars of the heavens).

> Then the angel of the Lord called to Abraham a second time from heaven, and said, **"By Myself I have sworn, declares the Lord, because you have done this thing and have not withheld your son, your only son, indeed I will greatly bless you, and I will greatly multiply your seed** as the stars of the heavens and as the sand which is on the seashore; and your seed shall possess the gate of their enemies."
>
> —Genesis 22:15-17

Abraham knew that He was making covenant with God Most High, and the loftiest King of all, King Melchizedek. Abraham's faith in God's promise brought a supernatural understanding that he was engaging in a heavenly trade and that he would end up with the greater blessing on his side of the trade. How right he was!

Mount Moriah was actually in Salem, which would later be named Jerusalem, the same place where Melchizedek was King and Priest of God Most High. This place had already been sanctified by the highest kingly and priestly government on earth. The pathway had already been prepared for Abraham by Melchizedek. He just had to follow it, and that is exactly what Abraham did. Jesus, our Melchizedek, has already paved the way for us when He chose the path of obedience even to the point of death on a cross. We just have to follow Him.

Threshing Floor

Mount Moriah is the same place where the second patriarch of the Melchizedek Order, King David (Psalm 110), would encounter God on a threshing floor.

> **Then the angel of the Lord commanded Gad to say to David, that David should go up and build an altar to the Lord on the threshing floor** of Ornan the Jebusite. So David went up at the word of Gad, which he spoke in the name of the Lord. Now Ornan turned back and saw the angel, and his four sons who were with him hid themselves. And Ornan was threshing wheat. As David came to Ornan, Ornan looked and saw David, and went out from the threshing floor and prostrated himself before David with his face to the ground. Then David said to Ornan, **"Give me the site of this threshing floor that I may build on it an altar to the Lord;** for the full price you shall give it to me, that the plague may be restrained from the people." Ornan said to David, "Take it for yourself; and let my lord the king do what is good in his sight. See, I will give the oxen for burnt offerings and the threshing sledges for wood and the wheat for the grain offering; I will give it all." But King David said to Ornan, **"No, but I will surely buy it for the full price; for I will not take what is yours for the Lord, or offer a burnt offering which costs me nothing."** So David gave Ornan 600 shekels of gold by weight for the site. Then David built an altar to the Lord there and offered burnt offerings and peace offerings. And

he called to the Lord and He answered him with
fire from heaven on the altar of burnt offering.
—1 Chronicles 21:18-26

The threshing floor is not an inexpensive pathway. This is a
place where what we give God costs us something. At this place
obedience may cost us everything. The threshing floor was actually
an altar of repentance for David. David could have received this
place for free, but he refused and said, "I will not offer God that
which costs me nothing." David paid 600 shekels of gold for the
site. A shekel of gold is worth about $500 today. If we do the math,
he paid about $300,000 for this place called the threshing floor of
Ornan. Plus, David bought the oxen for the sacrifice and the actual
threshing floor as well. You may say, "That was King David and he
was wealthy, so that was not really a big deal." But when is the last
time you met a wealthy person who wanted and insisted on paying
full price for something to the tune of more than $300,000? This
act of refusing to give God something that cost him nothing had
everything to do with why God answered him by fire from Heaven
on the altar of burnt offering. The greater the sacrifice, the more
power it has on the Trading Floor. It also had everything to do with
this threshing floor becoming the very place where there would be
unlimited resources and supply to fulfill David's destiny, making
preparation for a glorious house for his great God.

> **"Of the gold, the silver and the bronze and the
> iron there is no limit. Arise and work, and may
> the Lord be with you."**
> —1 Chronicles 22:16

There was no limit of supply to build David's dream house for
his God. How many of us have a dream to do something magnificent
for the Lord? Trading on the threshing floor or building an altar of
extravagant giving is actually the place where dreams in God come
true!

> Then Solomon began to build the house of the
> Lord in Jerusalem on Mount Moriah, where the
> Lord had appeared to his father David, at the place
> that David had prepared on the threshing floor of
> Ornan the Jebusite.
>
> —2 Chronicles 3:1

Abraham had already traded for this very building site to be made available to his descendants. This is the same site that was called Mount Moriah in Abraham's day. This is the same place that Abraham offered his promised son Isaac to the Lord by means of sacrifice about 1000 years before David was king. This same place was already sanctified and set apart as *Jehovah Jireh*, "The Lord will Provide"! When we embrace the hard places of God's leading, it not only releases a blessing to us, but it also releases blessings to the generations to follow. The blessing of Abraham goes forward to 1000 generations (Exodus 34 and Psalm 105)!

Not only was there limitless supply within Solomon's kingdom to build the temple, but it attracted wealth from outside the kingdom (wealth attracts wealth), as well. The queen of Sheba was drawn to this very place, arriving with camels laden with more wealth for the temple!

Camels

> Now when the queen of Sheba heard of the
> fame of Solomon, she came to Jerusalem to test
> Solomon with difficult questions. **She had a very
> large retinue, with camels carrying spices and a
> large amount of gold and precious stones; and
> when she came to Solomon, she spoke with him
> about all that was on her heart.**
>
> —2 Chronicles 9:1

The queen of Sheba showed up with camels and wealth to the same site of the threshing floor where Abraham and David sacrificed.

The word *camel* is *gamal* in Hebrew. *Gamal* means "**to deal bountifully with**, requite: make appropriate return for, to avenge, to pay someone back, to deal out to, to recompense, repay, etc."

Camels in the Bible were very frequently used as a symbol of wealth and abundance. We come to this understanding by considering the "Law of First Mention." This law implies that the very first time any significant word is mentioned in Scripture, that particular Scripture gives the word its most complete and accurate meaning, providing a foundation for future biblical use.

The first three appearances of the camel are coordinated with descriptions of the wealth of the first three patriarchs:

> **Therefore he treated Abram well for her sake;**
> **and gave him sheep and oxen and donkeys and**
> **male and female servants and female donkeys**
> **and camels.**
>
> —Genesis 12:16

> Then the servant took ten camels from the **camels**
> **of his master [Isaac], and set out with a variety**
> **of good things** of his master's in his hand; and
> he arose and went to Mesopotamia, to the city of
> Nahor.
>
> —Genesis 24:10

> **So the man [Jacob] became exceedingly**
> **prosperous**, and had large flocks and female and
> male servants and camels and donkeys.
>
> —Genesis 30:43

The queen of Sheba arrived at Solomon's temple (which was built on the threshing floor that David purchased for full price) with camels which represented great wealth.

Now when the queen of Sheba heard of the fame of Solomon, she came to Jerusalem to test Solomon with difficult questions. **She had a very large retinue, with camels carrying spices and a large amount of gold and precious stones;** and when she came to Solomon, she spoke with him about all that was on her heart.

—2 Chronicles 9:1

The Scripture tells us that there was a limitless supply of gold, silver, bronze and iron to build Solomon's temple. We see more abundant wealth shows up at a place that once was just a threshing floor on a mount. The patriarchs of our faith have paved the way for us to receive the same blessing. We are now the temple of the Lord, and God says that the latter glory of the temple (us) will be greater than the former glory.

"For thus says the Lord of hosts, 'Once more in a little while, I am going to shake the heavens and the earth, the sea also and the dry land. I will shake all the nations; **and they will come with the wealth of all nations, and I will fill this house with glory,**' says the Lord of hosts. **'The silver is Mine and the gold is Mine,**' declares the Lord of hosts. **'The latter glory of this house will be greater than the former,**' says the Lord of hosts, **'and in this place I will give peace,**' declares the Lord of hosts."

—Haggai 2:6-9

Although Zerubbabel's temple was not more glorious than Solomon's temple by means of appearance, it would indeed be a place of greater glory and honor. The Messiah Himself, the Lord Jesus Christ, would one day pick up the scroll of Isaiah 61 in Zerubbabel's temple and reveal Himself as the Messiah they had hoped and waited to encounter (Luke 4). We are the latter day temple of the Lord, and Jesus Christ, the hope of glory, dwells in us. The Lord will fill us with more of His glory as we embrace this place called the threshing floor. We, too, like Abraham and David, will have limitless supply to fulfill the dreams the Lord has placed within us.

In the previous chapter we discussed how Ruth found glorious redemption by embracing the threshing floor of Boaz in a place called the Shepherd's Field. This would be the same place where the angel would arrive to tell the shepherds how they could find their Savior, Christ the Lord.

> And this will be a sign for you [by which you will recognize Him]: you will find [after searching] a Baby **wrapped in swaddling clothes and lying in a manger.**
>
> —Luke 2:12 AMP

Swaddling clothes were used to wrap sacrificial lambs. There was only one place where lambs were wrapped in swaddling clothes; it was at the "Tower of the Flock" (called Migdal Edar) in the Shepherd's Field. That is why it was a sign to the shepherds to find the babe wrapped in swaddling clothes. They knew exactly where to go to find the Lamb of God who would take away the sins of the world. He would be found where all the other sacrificial lambs for Israel were found, in a manger wrapped in swaddling clothes.

> "As for you, tower of the flock, Hill of the daughter of Zion, to you it will come—even the former dominion will come, **the kingdom of the daughter of Jerusalem.**"
>
> —Micah 4:8

Beyond the Shepherd's Field to the east is the plain known to the Jewish people as the Field of Ruth. Jewish history tells us that this is the place where the Messiah would be born in the city of Bethlehem. This would be the same place to which the magi would travel from the east to bring the Child Jesus gold, frankincense and myrrh. In Jesus' day, people of importance rode on camels. Again, we see camels coming to the vicinity of a threshing floor (Boaz and Ruth's) with great treasures and wealth!

> Now after Jesus was born in Bethlehem of Judea
> in the days of Herod the king, **magi from the east**
> **arrived in Jerusalem, saying**, "Where is He who
> has been born King of the Jews? For we saw His
> star in the east and have come to worship Him."
> —Matthew 2:1-2

> After coming into the house they saw the Child
> with Mary His mother; and they fell to the
> ground and worshiped Him. **Then, opening their**
> **treasures, they presented to Him gifts of gold,**
> **frankincense, and myrrh.**
> —Matthew 2:11

The camels brought gold that symbolized wealth and the kingly dimension of the Order of Melchizedek, and the fact that Jesus was born King of the Jews. They also brought frankincense that was incense or perfume, symbolizing the priestly dimension of the Order of Melchizedek and the fact that Jesus was the High Priest forever in the Order of Melchizedek. And finally, they brought myrrh that was an embalming oil symbolizing that Jesus would lay His life down as a ransom for many. This also symbolized the governmental order of God's Kingdom, an eternal ancient order operating in the dimensions of both king and priest that would only manifest through death. The threshing floor is where all of these events took place, representing death to the flesh and death to self. It is not an easy place, but if we embrace it we will have traded for the authority to operate in the glorious priestly dimension of the Lord Jesus Christ, as well as His glorious kingly dimension. Death will bring abundant life! Abundant life will flow in our businesses and in our ministries as we operate in both dimensions as king and priest.

Isaiah 60

Magi came from the east with gifts. "From the east" actually means a **Rising of the Sun and Stars, Light Arising.**

Stars are going to rise and a light is going to shine!

> **"Arise, shine; for your light has come,**
> **And the glory of the Lord has risen upon you.**
> "For behold, darkness will cover the earth
> And deep darkness the peoples;
> But the Lord will rise upon you
> And His glory will appear upon you.
> "Nations will come to your light,
> And kings to the brightness of your rising.
> "Lift up your eyes round about and see;
> They all gather together, they come to you.
> Your sons will come from afar,
> And your daughters will be carried in the arms.
> "Then you will see and be radiant,
> And your heart will thrill and rejoice;
> Because the abundance of the sea will be turned to you,
> **The wealth of the nations will come to you.**
> **"A multitude of camels will cover you,**
> **The young camels of Midian and Ephah;**
> **All those from Sheba will come;**
> **They will bring gold and frankincense,**
> And will bear good news of the praises of the Lord.
> "All the flocks of Kedar will be gathered together to you,
> The rams of Nebaioth will minister to you;
> **They will go up with acceptance on My altar,**
> **And I shall glorify My glorious house.**
> "Who are these who fly like a cloud
> And like the doves to their lattices?
> "Surely the coastlands will wait for Me;
> **And the ships of Tarshish will come first,**

To bring your sons from afar,
Their silver and their gold with them,
For the name of the Lord your God,
And for the Holy One of Israel because
He has glorified you."

—Isaiah 60:1-9

The word *glory* in Isaiah 60:1, "The glory of the Lord has risen upon you," means abundance, riches, and glorious abundance! In verse 6 there is the promise that a multitude of camels will cover us! Prophetically speaking, the young camels of Midian will come and all the camels from Sheba are going to come as well. God is not finished with camels coming to His people from Sheba! The queen of Sheba showed up with camels laden down with wealth in Solomon's day. God is not finished with the commissioning from Sheba!

There is an interesting point I would like to make regarding the camels of Midian. These camels brought incredible wealth to the Israelites in the day of Gideon. Even more interestingly, Gideon was found threshing wheat in a wine press before he attained the incredible wealth from the camels of Midian. They are about to come again!

> Now it came about when the sons of Israel cried to
> the Lord on account of Midian, that the Lord sent
> a prophet to the sons of Israel, and he said to them,
> "Thus says the Lord, the God of Israel, 'It was I
> who brought you up from Egypt and brought you
> out from the house of slavery. I delivered you from
> the hands of the Egyptians and from the hands of
> all your oppressors, and dispossessed them before
> you and gave you their land, and I said to you, "I
> am the Lord your God; you shall not fear the gods
> of the Amorites in whose land you live. But you
> have not obeyed Me."'"Then the angel of the Lord
> came and sat under the oak that was in Ophrah,

which belonged to Joash the Abiezrite as his son
**Gideon was beating out wheat in the wine press
in order to save it from the Midianites.**
—Judges 6:7-11

Gideon is the judge God chooses to deliver the Israelites from the oppression of Midian.

Then the men of Israel said to Gideon, "Rule over us, both you and your son, also your son's son, **for you have delivered us from the hand of Midian."** But Gideon said to them, "I will not rule over you, nor shall my son rule over you; the Lord shall rule over you." Yet Gideon said to them, "I would request of you, that each of you give me an earring from his spoil." (For they had gold earrings, because they were Ishmaelites.) They said, "We will surely give them." So they spread out a garment, and every one of them threw an earring there from his spoil. **The weight of the gold earrings that he requested was 1,700 shekels of gold, besides the crescent ornaments and the pendants and the purple robes which were on the kings of Midian, and besides the neck bands (chains and pendants) that were on their camels' necks.**
—Judges 8:22-26

Gideon plundered the Midianites! According to my calculations, 1,700 shekels of gold would be equal to about $850,000 by today's standard, and that does not include the pendants, crescents and gold chains that were on the necks of the camels!

Gideon met God while he was threshing wheat in a wine press, but the end result of his obedience to the command of the Lord was deliverance and freedom for his nation. Instead of fear and poverty, he enjoyed extravagant wealth and great delight!

It is very important to note that in every case where the threshing floor was concerned, the key to victory was always obedience to the instruction of the Lord while on the threshing floor. The provision is hidden in the instruction and we will find it as we are embracing the threshing floor.

2013 (Hebrew year 5773) was prophetically named the "Year of the Camel" as the number three in Hebrew is *gimmel* (from the root, *gamal,* or camel). The Lord released the camels in 2013 and they will continue to be released and will manifest to those of us who have been trading obedience and death to self on the Trading Floor, which in this case is actually called the threshing floor! **The camels know exactly where to go. They always show up at the place where wheat was once threshed!**

And that is how Melchizedek, Threshing Floors, Camels and Isaiah 60 fit together!

LIFE APPLICATION SECTION

Memory Verse:

"Of the gold, the silver and the bronze and the iron there is no limit. Arise and work, and may the Lord be with you."

— 1 Chronicles 22:16

Reflections:

What is the priestly order of the Church of the Lord Jesus Christ?

_____

_____

_____

What do camels represent in Scripture?

_____

_____

_____

Where do camels always show up?

_____

_____

_____

JOURNAL YOUR THOUGHTS

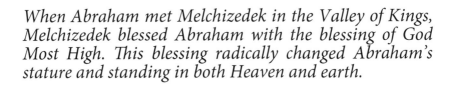

When Abraham met Melchizedek in the Valley of Kings, Melchizedek blessed Abraham with the blessing of God Most High. This blessing radically changed Abraham's stature and standing in both Heaven and earth.

Trading for a Lost Generation

Trading Floors, whether righteous or demonic, are places where we build altars of worship that bring dividends from the kingdom they represent.

In this chapter we are going to focus on the Kingdom of God and how we can become shareholders in the next great outpouring of the Holy Spirit that will precede the second coming of the Lord Jesus Christ.

A shareholder or stockholder is an individual or institution (including a corporation) that legally owns a share of stock in a public or private corporation. They buy shares which represent part ownership of a company.[1]

In our case, the company is our heavenly Father's Kingdom, the Kingdom of God. When Jesus was a young boy He stayed behind in the temple to discuss Scripture with the religious teachers of the day. When His parents finally found Him three days later, His response was, "Didn't you know that I would be about My Father's business?" The Kingdom of God is our Father's business, and righteous trading is legal and effective technology in building and expanding His business.

We can trade for anything we wish to have in the Kingdom of God. Right now, God is looking for those who are willing to trade for a lost generation.

The Spirit of Elijah

"For behold, the day is coming, burning like a
furnace; and all the arrogant and every evildoer
will be chaff; and the day that is coming will set
them ablaze," says the Lord of hosts, "so that it
will leave them neither root nor branch. But for
you who fear My name, the sun of righteousness
will rise with healing in its wings; and you will go
forth and skip about like calves from the stall. You
will tread down the wicked, for they will be ashes
under the soles of your feet on the day which I am
preparing," says the Lord of hosts.
"Remember the law of Moses My servant, even the
statutes and ordinances which I commanded him
in Horeb for all Israel.
**"Behold, I am going to send you Elijah the
prophet before the coming of the great and
terrible day of the Lord. He will restore the
hearts of the fathers to their children and the
hearts of the children to their fathers, so that I
will not come and smite the land with a curse."**
—Malachi 4:1-6

This was written in about 450 BC and here we are in 2014. Everywhere we look we can see that the land has been smitten with the "curse" of a fatherless generation. From this Scripture we can see that the spirit of Elijah is the antidote to purge the land of the curse. The spirit of Elijah will be what causes the great outpouring of the latter day rain to be released and will also prepare the way for the second coming of the Lord Jesus Christ.

In my opinion, the Prophet Elijah's greatest feat was slaying 450 prophets of Baal and 400 prophets of the Asherah:

> **When Ahab saw Elijah, Ahab said to him, "Is this you, you troubler of Israel?" He said, "I have not troubled Israel, but you and your father's house have, because you have forsaken the commandments of the Lord and you have followed the Baals. Now then send and gather to me all Israel at Mount Carmel, together with 450 prophets of Baal and 400 prophets of the Asherah, who eat at Jezebel's table."**
>
> —1 Kings 18:17-20

Ahab was angry with Elijah because Elijah prophesied that there would not be rain until he said so, which ended up being three and one-half years! By this time, the land was in great famine and everything was dying. There certainly was a curse upon the land. A closed heaven was taking its toll on everything and everyone in Israel. Why was this happening? It surely was not Elijah's fault as Ahab had implied. The fault belonged to Ahab and his ancestors, the kings of Israel, for forsaking the commandments of the Lord. They had worshiped Baal and the Asherah that were Jezebel's gods. Their prophets, 850 of them, were even eating at Jezebel's table at Israel's expense.

Evil Exposed

These three evil spirits, Baal, Asherah and Jezebel, still function together in our day. The altars that the heads of families have established in their homes to these ruling spirits are why we have so many broken homes, rebellious teenagers, teenage suicides and young girls enslaved in sex trafficking all over the world. The fathers of this generation have traded their children at the altars of these ruling spirits, with the head ruling spirit being Baal.

- Baal is identified as the ruler of the demons in Matthew 12:24. (Beelzebub is another name for Baal.)

- Baal-hamon, one of Baal's names, means "the lord of wealth or abundance."

- Baal-berith, another of his names, means "the lord of the covenant." The Hebrew word baal actually means "husband" or "marriage." This spirit always attempted to cause Israel to "divorce" or break covenant with God and "marry" or align with him. Consistent with this, in so many ways America has broken covenant with God and married Baal. This is, I believe, the strongman behind most covenant-breaking.

- Baal always goes after the next generation, trying to cut off the extension of God's covenantal purposes.

- Baal is leading the fight to avert the great awakening planned for the young generation of Americans today.[2]

Worship of Asherah was noted for its sensuality and prostitution (2 Kings 23:7).

Jezebel is a spirit in the Church that teaches and leads the Lord's bond-servants astray so that they commit acts of immorality (Revelation 2:20).

According to statistics, the divorce rate is about the same for those who attend church and those who do not attend church.

Countless servants of God have already gone astray and many more will do the same if the spirit of Elijah doesn't come forth. Innumerable fathers, even in the Church of the Lord Jesus Christ, have traded their wives and children on the altars of Baal for wealth or temporary sexual pleasures. Many years ago my children and I were victims of such a trade. We were traded by my children's biological father on the demonic altar of Baal and the tremendous pain almost cost my then ten-year-old son his life.

The spirit behind the fatherlessness in our nation and the nations of the world is Baal. The same strong man is after the current generation of young people. The land has been smitten with a curse and the ONLY antidote is the spirit of Elijah, Jezebel's greatest enemy!

Elijah's Precise Strategy

Elijah didn't just decide to challenge the prophets of Baal and Asherah to a showdown of spiritual power because he was bored one day and thought it would be a fun thing to do to kill time during the drought. No, Elijah had a precise strategy from the Lord. The strategy he used nearly 3,000 years ago to take down 450 prophets of Baal and 400 prophets of Asherah is just as effective today. Let's look at the strategy he used when he challenged the prophets of Baal and Asherah to a showdown on Mount Carmel. The God who answered and consumed the sacrifice by fire would be known as the true and living God!

> "Now then send and gather to me all Israel at
> Mount Carmel, together with 450 prophets of Baal
> and 400 prophets of the Asherah,
> who eat at Jezebel's table."
> **So Ahab sent a message among all the sons
> of Israel and brought the prophets together
> at Mount Carmel. Elijah came near to all the
> people and said, "How long will you hesitate
> between two opinions? If the Lord is God, follow
> Him; but if Baal, follow him."** But the people
> did not answer him a word. Then Elijah said to

the people, "I alone am left a prophet of the Lord,
but Baal's prophets are 450 men. Now let them
give us two oxen; and let them choose one ox
for themselves and cut it up, and place it on the
wood, but put no fire under it; and I will prepare
the other ox and lay it on the wood, and I will not
put a fire under it. Then you call on the name of
your god, and I will call on the name of the Lord,
and the God who answers by fire, He is God." And
all the people said, "That is a good idea."
                                        —1 Kings 18:19-24

This was a monumental moment in the history of the nation of Israel. The people had lost their strong convictions and faith in the God of Israel due to the sins of their fathers and the national leaders. Does that sound like where we are today in America and many nations of the world? This generation has no idea who God is and they vacillate between two opinions. They want to believe in God, yet they wonder if He is for real. They have been wounded by hurtful experiences in their family life and are confused by what they observe being worshiped by national leaders and stars in the media.

So Elijah said to the prophets of Baal, "Choose
one ox for yourselves and prepare it first for you
are many, and call on the name of your god,
but put no fire under it." Then they took the ox
which was given them and they prepared it and
called on the name of Baal from morning until
noon saying, "O Baal, answer us." But there was
no voice and no one answered. And they leaped
about the altar which they made. **It came about at
noon, that Elijah mocked them and said, "Call
out with a loud voice, for he is a god; either he
is occupied or gone aside, or is on a journey, or
perhaps he is asleep and needs to be awakened."**

So they cried with a loud voice and cut themselves
according to their custom with swords and
lances until the blood gushed out on them. When
midday was past, they raved until the time of
the offering of the evening sacrifice; but there
was no voice, no one answered, and no one paid
attention.

—1 Kings 18:25-29

Elijah had been making a mockery of Baal long before the
showdown on Mount Carmel. Baal was the god of productivity.
He was the farm god and he was to bring increase to families.
Three and one-half years earlier the Prophet Elijah told Ahab that
there would be no rain until he said so. So much for Baal, the god
of productivity! No rain for three and one-half years equals great
drought, no harvest, and great famine! Ahab was so angry with
Elijah for pronouncing this drought that he plotted to kill him.
Elijah was sent to hide by a brook and a raven brought him food.
When the brook dried up he was then sent to a widow who was
preparing to make her final cake and die with her son. However,
she gave her last cake to Elijah and the flour and water that she
used did not give out until the drought was over. We see that a
very severe drought was already in place because of the power of
Elijah's words. Baal, Asherah, Jezebel and 850 false prophets were
completely powerless to compete against the God of Israel and His
one true prophet, Elijah. Mount Carmel was going to be the final
showdown!

Repair the Altar of the Lord

Then Elijah said to all the people, "Come near to
me." So all the people came near to him. **And he
repaired the altar of the Lord which had been
torn down.**

—1 Kings 18:30

This is the first step that must be taken if we desire to bring healing to this generation and usher in the release of the spirit of Elijah that will turn the hearts of the children to the fathers and the fathers to the children. We need to repair the altars that have been torn down. Many people bow their knee and sacrifice to the god of Baal, the god of productivity. They trade their families on the altar of Baal for wealth. They do not have time to build an altar to the Lord because they are too busy chasing wealth. We cannot serve God and money. Listen to what Jesus said,

> "No one can serve two masters; for either he will
> hate the one and love the other, or he will be
> devoted to one and despise the other. **You cannot
> serve God and wealth.**"
> —Matthew 6:24

Anytime we put financial increase before God we are building an altar to Baal. Many people have traded their families at that altar, even those in the Church of the Lord Jesus Christ.

We should all have a personal altar of worship to the Lord, even if it is the dash board of our car on our way to work in the morning. An altar is actually positioned on a Trading Floor. It is where we sacrifice our time to be with God and He grants us the answers to our prayers and the blessings and provisions of His Kingdom. We should also have family altars, where we spend time with God as a family. These altars of worship and sacrifice alone will begin to release the spirit of Elijah and will begin to bring healing and deliverance to this generation.

Build New Altars

**Elijah took twelve stones according to the
number of the tribes of the sons of Jacob, to
whom the word of the Lord had come, saying,**

"Israel shall be your name." So with the stones he
built an altar in the name of the Lord ...
—1 Kings 18: 31-32

The name *Israel* means "God prevails"!

We see that Elijah not only repaired the altars that were torn
down from the past but he built a new altar with twelve stones. Twelve
is the number of perfect government. God's perfect government is the
Order of Melchizedek (Isaiah 9). The Order of Melchizedek turns the
hearts of the fathers to the children and the children to the fathers.
The spiritual technology is built into the ancient Melchizedek Order
itself because it was authorized by God the Father and God the Son
(Psalm 110). This is the government of the Kingdom of God for the
dispensation of time that we live in today (Hebrews 5-8).

Dig Deep

So with the stones he built an altar in the name of
the Lord, and he made a trench around the altar,
large enough to hold two measures of seed.
—1 Kings 18:32

The next thing Elijah did was make a trench. He dug deep into
the earth to make enough room for two measures of seed, not just
one! Remember, Elijah was expecting God to answer by fire, so he
needed to make sure this trade on the altar would be significant
enough for God to answer by fire and for the fire to be big enough
to save a generation. Elijah was after the entire generation of Israel
and he was willing to sacrifice enough time, effort and seed to
make sure he got what he was trading for.

Always remember, the greater the sacrifice, the more power it
has on the Trading Floor.

Sometimes we need to dig deep within our own "earthen
vessels" to remove the old in order to make room for the new.
That is also an acceptable trade before God!

Take Up the Cross

Then he arranged the wood and cut the ox in
pieces and laid it on the wood.
—1 Kings 18:33

The next thing Elijah did was arrange the wood. That would
symbolize the cross of Jesus.

And He was saying to them all, "If anyone wishes
to come after Me, he must deny himself, **and take
up his cross daily and follow Me."**
—Luke 9:23

The altar of fire that will save a generation must be a place
of death to self. The Apostle Paul said, "I die daily." Paul had to
die daily so that others could live. He was well rewarded for his
sacrificial trade. God gave him the honor of writing two-thirds of
the New Testament and he is recorded in history as one of the
greatest men of God that ever lived. We never give God more than
He gives back to us on His Trading Floor!

Then he arranged the wood and **cut the ox in
pieces and laid it** on the wood.
—1 Kings 18:33

The ox cut in pieces and placed on the wood symbolizes man
on the cross. We trade our strength for His, all that we are for all
that He is.

Therefore I urge you, brethren, by the mercies
of God, **to present your bodies a living and
holy sacrifice,** acceptable to God, which is your
spiritual service of worship.
—Romans 12:1

Submit to God's Government

> And he said, **"Fill four pitchers with water and
> pour it on the burnt offering and on the wood."**
> And he said, "Do it a second time," and they did
> it a second time. And he said, "Do it a third time,"
> and they did it a third time.
>
> —1 Kings 18:34

Notice the next thing Elijah did was pour water over the sacrifice. Three times he poured four pitchers of water over the sacrifice, a total of twelve, symbolic of God's perfect government. God's government will always bring about power but it will not be established without repentance. Repentance comes first. John the Baptist came before God's government, the Lord Jesus Christ.

Repentance always precedes a significant move of God's government; that is why John the Baptist had to come before Jesus. The Jewish people did not believe that Jesus was the Messiah because they were taught that Elijah would return before the Messiah would appear. What they didn't realize is that the spirit and power of Elijah had already appeared in the life of John the Baptist.

Elijah Appeared in John

> They asked Him, saying, **"Why is it that the
> scribes say that Elijah must come first?" And
> He said to them, "Elijah does first come and
> restore all things.** And yet how is it written of
> the Son of Man that He will suffer many things
> and be treated with contempt? **But I say to you
> that Elijah has indeed come, and they did to
> him whatever they wished, just as it is written of
> him."**
>
> —Mark 9:11-13

John the Baptist was the voice of one crying in the wilderness to prepare the way of the Lord's first coming. His voice was a voice of repentance, and that is exactly what the water over Elijah's sacrifice represented, repentance.

> As these men were going away, Jesus began to speak to the crowds about John, "What did you go out into the wilderness to see? A reed shaken by the wind? But what did you go out to see? A man dressed in soft clothing? Those who wear soft clothing are in kings' palaces! But what did you go out to see? A prophet? Yes, I tell you, and one who is more than a prophet. This is the one about whom it is written, **'Behold, I send My messenger ahead of You, Who will prepare Your way before You.'** Truly I say to you, among those born of women there has not arisen anyone greater than John the Baptist! Yet the one who is least in the kingdom of heaven is greater than he. **From the days of John the Baptist until now the kingdom of heaven suffers violence, and violent men take it by force.** For all the prophets and the Law prophesied until John. And if you are willing to accept it, **John himself is Elijah who was to come. He who has ears to hear, let him hear."**
> —Matthew 11:7-15

God is looking for His messengers who will prepare His way and restore all things before He returns.

The Kingdom of God suffers violence and violent men take it by force. Elijah and John both took a violent stance against sin. If we want the same Spirit they had to be released in our day, then we will have to be violent against sin as well, especially the sin of Baal (the worship of productivity, money, and wealth), the sin of Asherah (sexual perversion), and Jezebel (control, witchcraft, rebellion and sexual immorality).

We must not tolerate these evil forces. Both Elijah and John were confrontational towards sin.

We must beware of exposing ourselves or our families to the perverse spirits in certain TV programs or in movie theaters, causing us to compromise by tolerating evil. We must not allow the seed of the enemy to come into our eye and ear gates (words and pictures are seeds that come in through our gates), because we will then have mixed seed inside of us. This is a picture of harlotry because we are taking in the world's seed rather than the Lord Jesus Christ's seed of truth revealed by the Holy Spirit and the Word of God.

I realize this is strong, but if we are going to save a generation we need to heed the wakeup call before it is too late and we are held accountable before the Lord for a lost generation. We want to offer the Lord pure fire, not "strange fire" like Aaron's sons offered (Leviticus 10:1).

Remember what Jesus had against the church of Thyatira?

> "But I have this against you, **that you tolerate the woman Jezebel,** who calls herself a prophetess, and she teaches and leads My bond-servants astray so that they commit acts of immorality and eat things sacrificed to idols."
>
> —Revelation 2:20

Do we really want the Lord Jesus Christ to hold something against us? He may, if we continue to tolerate Jezebel and her force of immorality in our nation. It is time for the Church to repent for compromising and turning a blind eye to these evil forces.

The spirit of Jezebel hates repentance, because it knows the immense damage repentance does to the Kingdom of Darkness and what explosion it brings to the Kingdom of Light. Herodias, moved by the spirit of Jezebel, was the one who had John the Baptist beheaded because he confronted her sin and told her to repent. John was confrontational and Jesus said that there was no one greater than John. We will not be able to please both God and man. I believe it is time for us to make a choice.

Water of Repentance

Elijah, just like John the Baptist, prepared the way for God's revival FIRE...a pure and holy fire that would save a generation. The water of repentance precedes revival fire!

> **The water flowed around the altar and he also filled the trench with water.**
> —1 Kings 18:35

> "As for me, **I baptize you with water for repentance,** but He who is coming after me is mightier than I, and I am not fit to remove His sandals; **He will baptize you with the Holy Spirit and fire. His winnowing fork is in His hand, and He will thoroughly clear His threshing floor; and He will gather His wheat into the barn, but He will burn up the chaff with unquenchable fire."**
> —Matthew 3:11-12

The Scripture makes it clear: First repentance, as demonstrated by Elijah and John through water baptism, then the Holy Spirit and fire.

> "I baptized you with water; but He will baptize you with the Holy Spirit." In those days Jesus came from Nazareth in Galilee and was baptized by John in the Jordan. **Immediately coming up**

**out of the water, He saw the heavens opening,
and the Spirit like a dove descending upon Him;
and a voice came out of the heavens:** "You are
My beloved Son, in You I am well-pleased."

—Mark 1:8-11

The picture is so clear: John baptized with water for repentance; the repentance brought Jesus on the scene (God's governmental Order of Melchizedek in flesh and blood). Then the heavens opened and God spoke. Three years later on the day of Pentecost the baptism of fire came and 3,000 souls were saved during Peter's first message! Peter was a messenger of repentance. Read the account of his message in Acts 2-3.

**"Therefore repent and return, so that your
sins may be wiped away, in order that times of
refreshing may come from the presence of the
Lord; and that He may send Jesus, the Christ
appointed for you."**

—Acts 3:19-20

Repentance brings times of refreshing. It also brings Jesus the Christ, appointed for us in our time of need. If we need Jesus Christ to show up in our lives and in the lives of our families and this generation, then we need to embrace repentance because repentance brings Jesus, the Christ appointed!

Change of Mind

Repent means to change one's mind for the better. It does not mean that we go around saying, "I repent, I repent, I repent." It means that we change our mind and go in a different direction for the better, which is the direction of the cross (the ox on the wooden altar).

At the time of the offering of the evening sacrifice,
Elijah the prophet came near and said, "O Lord,

the God of Abraham, Isaac and Israel, today let
it be known that You are God in Israel and that I
am Your servant and I have done all these things
at Your word. **Answer me, O Lord, answer me,
that this people may know that You, O Lord, are
God, and that You have turned their heart back
again."**

—1 Kings 18:36-37

Elijah's entire purpose was to save the lost generation of Israel.
He wanted to see the people's hearts return to God. He wanted to
see them change their minds so they would no longer be swayed
between the voice of Baal (world) and the voice of the true and
living God.

**Then the fire of the Lord fell and consumed the
burnt offering** and the wood and the stones and
the dust, and licked up the water that was in the
trench. **When all the people saw it, they fell on
their faces; and they said, "The Lord, He is God;
the Lord, He is God."**

—1 Kings 18:38-39

God honored each and every strategic step that Elijah took on
Mount Carmel that day. God answered by fire, and everyone knew
from that day forward that the God of Israel was the only true and
living God. Revival fire came and the nation was restored back to
God!

But that is not all!

Authority to Reign

Then Elijah said to them, "Seize the prophets
of Baal; do not let one of them escape." **So they**

seized them; and Elijah brought them down to the brook Kishon, and slew them there.

—1 Kings 18:40

What an amazing feat by ONE true prophet of God. It is interesting to note that Jesus said John the Baptist was the Elijah who was to come, and that of those born of women none were greater than John. But Jesus went on even further to say that those who are in the Kingdom are greater than John. So John was greater than Elijah and we are greater than Elijah and John! You see, Elijah slew the prophets of Baal but it was Jehu the king of Israel who crushed Jezebel. Elijah didn't have a kingly anointing and it would take a kingly anointing to deal with the spirit of Jezebel. John the Baptist did not destroy Herodias because his anointing was that of a priest and prophet, not a king and priest. But in the New Covenant we are both kings and priests unto the Most High God under the Order of Melchizedek. All that is necessary to dismantle this evil trio, Baal, Asherah and Jezebel, has been set in order by God's government. All the authority and power of the Godhead has been invested in the Order of Melchizedek.

When they saw Him, they worshiped Him; but some were doubtful. And Jesus came up and spoke to them, saying, **"All authority has been given to Me in heaven and on earth. Go therefore and make disciples of all the nations,** baptizing them in the name of the Father and the Son and the Holy Spirit."

—Matthew 28:17-19

"Behold, I have given you authority to tread on serpents and scorpions, and over all the power of the enemy, and nothing will injure you."

—Luke 10:19

We have all authority over the enemy as long as we do not have anything in common with the enemy. That is the great key to victory! Repentance and applying the blood of Jesus will deliver us from having anything in common with him. If he can find something in us that is "common ground," we will be defeated every time.

No Common Ground

Jesus said, *"The god of this world comes **but he has nothing in me"** (John 14:30).

Moses had to wait until he was standing on "holy ground" before he could go back and dispossess the ungodly nation of Egypt. He could have nothing left in common with the gods of Egypt or he would have failed his mission.

Holy means "set apart for (uncommon) use." *Profane* actually means "common." Lucifer was cast out of God's sight because he was profaning the sanctuary of God. He was making it a common place. The most important rule of engagement in spiritual warfare is sanctification and consecration. It took Moses forty years to become totally free from the influences of Egypt.

Joshua and all of Israel had to go through consecration and circumcision before the Angel of the Lord showed up to do battle with them at Jericho. Once they were completely consecrated, the Lord told Joshua that he was standing on holy ground. Once Joshua was standing on holy ground, the Angel of the Lord drew His sword and was ready to do battle for the nation (Joshua 5-6).

After Jericho, they lost the battle at Ai because they picked up something in common with the land of Ai (Joshua 7). So again, the most important rule of engagement is having nothing in common with the sin of the land, otherwise we will be ineffective.

False Trinity

The Lord revealed to me that this combination of evil spirits, Baal, Asherah and Jezebel, stick together. They stand together as the "false trinity" of the Kingdom of Darkness. Satan is known to mimic God in every way and any way that he can, so this should not surprise us.

Baal is the ruler of the false trinity and one of his names means "Lord of the Covenant." The symbol for the Asherah is a wooden pole. Jezebel calls herself a prophetess and teaches and leads God's people to go astray.

Father God is a God of Covenant. Jesus died on a wooden cross. The Holy Spirit is the one who leads us and teaches us in the way of truth.

> And if one can overpower him who is alone, two
> can resist him. **A cord of three strands** is not
> quickly torn apart.
> —Ecclesiastes 4:12

Satan understands that a threefold cord cannot easily be broken. He commissioned these three evil spirits to stay together with the goal of destroying families, the next generation, and ultimately causing the covenant that God has with His children to be broken.

When the Lord told me that my children and I had been legally traded on the altar of Baal, I felt like I had some unfinished business to take care of, even though it happened many years before and my former husband had since repented and made things right with my children and me. In light of the new revelation, I felt that I needed to set things straight with the enemy.

Setting Things Straight

By the way, it is important to remember that our parents and former spouses are not the enemy; they are victims of the trade, as well. People are never the force we fight against.

For our struggle is not against flesh and blood, but against the rulers, against the powers, against the world forces of this darkness, against the spiritual forces of wickedness in the heavenly places. Therefore, take up the full armor of God, so that you will be able to resist in the evil day, and having done everything, to stand firm.
—Ephesians 6:12-13

This is how the Holy Spirit led me to pray:

- I repented for myself and my ancestors for any Baal or idol worship (Nehemiah 9:2).

- I cleansed my bloodline of anything and everything to do with the love of money, sexual perversion, witchcraft and immorality through more repentance and application of the blood of Jesus (Revelation 12).

- I forgave and released my former husband for trading us on Baal's altar and asked God to forgive him (John 20:23).

- I renounced the three false gods, smashed their altars and cut up the Asherah pole and commanded it to be burned (Judges 6:25-26).

- I cut the cord (Psalm 129:4) that bound them together, with the sword of the Lord that is filled with His blood (Isaiah 34:6).

- I bound them with God's fetters and chains of iron (Psalm 149).

- I commanded that their thrones be overthrown in the Name of Jesus (Haggai 2:22).

- I exalted the Lord and His throne by entering into high praises (Psalms 22 and 149).

- I set up a new altar of consecration to the Lord for my family in the place of the demonic altar (1 Kings 18:32).

- I also stripped off any residue of the enemy's false identity from myself and my children and called forth the full identity that we were to have in Christ Jesus (1 Peter 2:9).

- I commanded full restitution for everything lost and stolen (Proverbs 6:31).

- I commanded time to be redeemed and all time barriers to collapse and be destroyed in the fire of God (Ephesians 1:7).

I am not implying this is the only way to pray, as I am not much into prayer formulas. Taking dominion over the enemy's diabolical assignments against you and your children is most important. The enemy has already been defeated by the death, burial and resurrection of the Lord Jesus Christ. Basically, we need to enforce the victory of the cross. Once the revelation (light) comes, darkness is destroyed.

Legal Trade

The point is that God was teaching me the principles of spiritual trading. He wanted me to understand that a legal trade was transacted in the spirit realm on the day that my former husband put us on the altar of Baal. He legally gave us up for other pleasures that the enemy would offer him in place of us. The enemy said, "You can have my property and I'll take yours." Remember, the enemy is always out to make a trade. He was a trader from the beginning and he always demands something in return for the use of Sin's Intellectual Property. The enemy then claimed my children and me as his legal territory. His mission was to steal our identity in God and pervert the destiny that God had chosen for us from the foundation of the world, which was written on our original scrolls in Heaven.

> Your eyes have seen my unformed substance; **and in Your book were all written the days that were ordained for me,** when as yet there was not one of them.
>
> —Psalm 139:16

We were once a Christian family, but now sold on the altars of Baal. Christian families, especially those with immense calls of God on their lives, bring the highest dividends to the Kingdom of Darkness. We went through a season of very intense warfare but the gates of hell could not prevail against us. The Lion from the Tribe of Judah had already triumphed on our behalf! We belong to Him alone and God has caused all things to work together for our good!

Healing in His Wings

If you have been traded on the altars of Baal by a parent or spouse, just ask the Lord for the wisdom and the strategy to dismantle the enemy's stronghold. The steps might be different for you, but I believe that the Holy Spirit will lead each and every one who reads this book into absolute freedom and full restitution of lost time and stolen property. There is healing for those of us who fear His Name.

> **"But for you who fear My name, the sun of righteousness will rise with healing in its wings; and you will go forth and skip about like calves from the stall. You will tread down the wicked, for they will be ashes under the soles of your feet on the day which I am preparing," says the Lord of hosts.**
>
> —Malachi 4:2-3

It is time to pursue, overtake and recover all that was lost on the Trading Floor of Darkness!

Elijah's story does not end there; there is more good news!

Elijah Births Rain

Now Elijah said to Ahab, "Go up, eat and drink; for there is the sound of the roar of a heavy shower." So Ahab went up to eat and drink. **But Elijah went up to the top of Carmel; and he crouched down on the earth and put his face between his knees.** He said to his servant, "Go up now, look toward the sea." So he went up and looked and said, "There is nothing." And he said, "Go back" seven times. It came about at the seventh time, that he said, "Behold, a cloud as small as a man's hand is coming up from the sea." And he said, "Go up, say to Ahab, 'Prepare your chariot and go down, so that the heavy shower does not stop you.'" **In a little while the sky grew black with clouds and wind, and there was a heavy shower.** And Ahab rode and went to Jezreel. Then the hand of the Lord was on Elijah, and he girded up his loins and outran Ahab to Jezreel.
—1 Kings 18:41-46

Not only did Elijah slay all the wicked false prophets but afterwards he birthed a season of rain! Rain always symbolizes the rain of God's Presence! Elijah birthed a new season for Israel and for the next generation.

Elijah was a man with a nature like ours, and he prayed earnestly that it would not rain, and it did not rain on the earth for three years and six months.

—James 5:17

Elijah was a man just like us! If he could stop rain and then birth rain with earnest prayer as an Old Testament prophet, how much more can be done with earnest prayer under the Order of Melchizedek?

Authority of the Order

The Lord says to my Lord:
"Sit at My right hand
**Until I make Your enemies
a footstool for Your feet."
The Lord will stretch forth
Your strong scepter from Zion, saying,
"Rule in the midst of Your enemies."**
Your people will volunteer freely
in the **day of Your power;**
In holy array, from the womb of the dawn,
**Your youth are to You as the dew [the next
generation]. The Lord has sworn
and will not change His mind,
"You are a priest forever
According to the order of Melchizedek."**
The Lord is at Your right hand;
He will shatter kings in the day of His wrath.
He will judge among the nations,
He will fill them with corpses,
He will shatter the chief men over a broad country.
He will drink from the brook by the wayside;
Therefore He will lift up His head.

—Psalm 110

This is the day of His power and these are the days of Elijah!

Authority over the Nations

"He who overcomes, and he who keeps My deeds until the end, to him I will give authority over the nations; and he shall rule them with a rod of iron, as the vessels of the potter are broken to pieces, as I also have received authority from My Father; and I will give him the morning star."

—Revelation 2:26-28

This is the promise for all of us who are willing to climb our mountain and trade on the altars of self-sacrifice and repentance like Elijah did. We will be shareholders in the next move of God's Spirit. The move will save a lost generation. It will move into all the nations of the world and the hearts of the fathers will be turned to the children and the children to the fathers. Every land will be healed of the curse of the fatherless generation and the way will be prepared for the Lord's return!

LIFE APPLICATION SECTION

Memory Verse:

Then the fire of the Lord fell and consumed the burnt offering and the wood and the stones and the dust, and licked up the water that was in the trench. When all the people saw it, they fell on their faces; and they said, "The Lord, He is God; the Lord, He is God."

—1 Kings 18:38-46

Reflections:

What was the first thing Elijah did when he challenged the false prophets?

_____

_____

_____

What will bring the Presence of the Lord, the Christ appointed to you?

_____

_____

_____

What spirit will turn the hearts of the fathers to the children and the children to the fathers?

_____

_____

_____

JOURNAL YOUR THOUGHTS

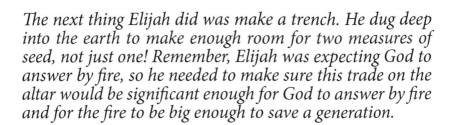

The next thing Elijah did was make a trench. He dug deep into the earth to make enough room for two measures of seed, not just one! Remember, Elijah was expecting God to answer by fire, so he needed to make sure this trade on the altar would be significant enough for God to answer by fire and for the fire to be big enough to save a generation.

10

PLUNDERING THE ENEMY'S TRADING FLOOR

In Chapter 4, *The King of Sodom and the End-Time Wealth Transfer*, I touched on how to plunder the enemy's Trading Floor. This chapter will be a more in-depth view.

The blood of the Lord Jesus Christ, when appropriated with repentance, is the only thing powerful enough to plunder the enemy's Trading Floor. Yes, the blood of Jesus answers all the demands of Satan regarding the unrighteous trades that have been made by us and our former generations.

The Blood Answers Every Demand

"Come now, and let us reason together,"
Says the Lord, **"Though your sins are as scarlet,**
They will be as white as snow;
Though they are red like crimson,
They will be like wool."

—Isaiah 1:18

"I, even I, am the one who wipes out your
transgressions for My own sake,
And I will not remember your sins.
"Put Me in remembrance,
let us argue our case together;
State your cause, that you may be proved right.
"Your first forefather sinned,
And your spokesmen have
transgressed against Me.
"So I will pollute the princes of the sanctuary,
And I will consign Jacob to the ban and Israel to
revilement."

—Isaiah 43:25-28

We can see that for God's own sake He wants to wipe out our transgressions. He does not want to remember our sins. That is the heart of our Father God. He wants to bless us and heal us. His desire is for us to prosper and be in health, even as our souls prosper. He wants the very best for us. His desire to bless us, His children, far exceeds what we could even imagine. He wants to bless us more than we want to bless our own natural and spiritual children. However, God is not only our Father; He is also a Righteous Judge. Even though it is in His Father's heart to bless us, God will never compromise Himself as Righteous Judge. God requires repentance and the blood of His Son Jesus, our Messiah, to bring everything into legal judicial order in the courts of Heaven.

There Are Many Books in Heaven

There are many books in Heaven. Everything is recorded, especially regarding righteous and unrighteous trading. What has been written about us and our past generations greatly affects our lives on earth. That is why these legal decrees against us must be blotted out or wiped out of the books. The blood of Jesus is the supernatural eraser!

Satan has to have legal right to bring charges against us. Our goal is to take away every legal stance he has against us and our children, as well as those for whom we intercede. Everything concerning trading has legal implications. Legal implications are the consequences of our actions as determined by law. There are books in the courts of Heaven. Our goal is to have the legal accusations and hostile decrees which are written in them regarding illegal trades, blotted out! Satan roams to and fro on the earth watching everything that is happening. He knows the contents of those books and accuses us accordingly (Revelation 12:10).

> "A river of fire was flowing
> And coming out from before Him;
> Thousands upon thousands were attending Him,
> And myriads upon myriads were standing before
> Him; **The court sat, and the books were opened."**
> —Daniel 7:10

> And I saw the dead, the great and the small,
> standing before the throne, **and books were
> opened; and another book was opened, which
> is the book of life; and the dead were judged
> from the things which were written in the books,
> according to their deeds.**
> —Revelation 20:12

Sins of the Forefathers

The Bible teaches us that God is merciful and full of loving-kindness. He readily forgives sin in keeping with His Father's heart, but He also requires that the guilty be punished. He visits the sins of the forefathers to the third and fourth generations of all that hate him because He is the Righteous Judge. To those who turn to Him, He visits the generations with the hope of deliverance and the promise of redemption through repentance.

> Then the LORD passed by in front of him
> and proclaimed, "The LORD, the LORD God,
> compassionate and gracious, slow to anger, and
> abounding in lovingkindness and truth; who
> keeps loving kindness for thousands, who forgives
> iniquity, transgression and sin; **yet He will by
> no means leave the guilty unpunished, visiting
> the iniquity of fathers on the children and
> on the grandchildren to the third and fourth
> generations."**
>
> —Exodus 34:6-7

Here's the situation: Not only do we want God to wipe out our illegal trades, but also those of the former four generations before us. According to the Word of God, illegal trading can go back as far as four generations. (I highly recommend reading *Breaking Generational Curses Under the Order of Melchizedek* by Dr. Francis Myles.)

In Isaiah 43 we read, *"Your first forefather sinned, and your spokesmen have transgressed against me. So I will pollute the princes of the sanctuary; and I will consign Jacob to the ban, and Israel to revilement"* (verses 27-28). That was the open door to the curses and reproaches that followed. Even though God wants to wipe out everything that stands against Israel in the courts of Heaven, there is a sin issue that needs to be dealt with. Notice that God does not address their own sin but the sin of their forefathers and their spokesmen, which would be spiritual leaders such as teachers and priests. In Chapter 4 we discussed how the sins of our leaders can have great impact on our lives.

Repentance Is Key to Deliverance

The Bible speaks of repentance, not only for our sins but for the sins of our ancestors and our spiritual leaders. That is the key to plundering the Trading Floor of the enemy.

> "When they sin against You (for there is no man who does not sin) and You are angry with them and deliver them to an enemy, so that they take them away captive to a land far off or near, **if they take thought in the land where they are taken captive, and repent and make supplication to You in the land of their captivity, saying, 'We have sinned, we have committed iniquity and have acted wickedly'; if they return to You with all their heart and with all their soul in the land of their captivity, where they have been taken captive, and pray toward their land which You have given to their fathers and the city which You have chosen, and toward the house which I have built for Your name, then hear from heaven, from Your dwelling place, their prayer and supplications, and maintain their cause and forgive Your people who have sinned against You."**
>
> —2 Chronicles 6:36-39

> Then the Lord appeared to Solomon at night and said to him, "I have heard your prayer and have chosen this place for Myself as a house of sacrifice. **If I shut up the heavens so that there is no rain, or if I command the locust to devour the land,**

**or if I send pestilence among My people, and
My people who are called by My name humble
themselves and pray and seek My face and turn
from their wicked ways, then I will hear from
heaven, will forgive their sin and will heal their
land.”**

—2 Chronicles 7:12-14

Clearly the answer to healing our land (our family, nation and the nations) is repentance.

When the nation of Israel was plundered by foreign nations the answer was again repentance, not only in repenting for themselves, but for their forefathers and leaders who sinned against the Lord as well.

I said, “I beseech You, O LORD God of heaven,
the great and awesome God, who preserves the
covenant and loving kindness for those who love
Him and keep His commandments, let Your ear
now be attentive and Your eyes open to hear the
prayer of Your servant which I am praying before
You now, day and night, on behalf of the sons
of Israel Your servants, **confessing the sins of
the sons of Israel which we have sinned against
You; I and my father’s house have sinned.”**

—Nehemiah 1:5-6

Although the Jews completed the temple in 515 BC the city walls remained in shambles for the next 70 years. Nehemiah was able to bring the nation of Israel to a place of repentance, and because of this the walls of Jerusalem were rebuilt in just 52 days! After 140 years of being torn down, the walls that represented power, protection and beauty were all restored within just 52 days! Think about that for a minute, 140 years of destruction, completely restored in less than two months after confession and repentance were granted! Repentance does amazing things in a very short amount of time. It grants God the ability to bless and not judge. His heart is to heal and restore. The propitiation of the blood of Jesus gives God the legal right to bless us according to His own laws and judicial statutes.

A Kingdom of Priests

We must apply the blood as priests before we can plunder the enemy's Trading Floor as kings! We must first ensure everything is taken care of legally in the courts of Heaven. We do this as priests under the Order of Melchizedek by appropriating the blood of Jesus as the Holy Spirit directs us. Once the accusations are silenced with the blood of Jesus, then we can plunder the Trading Floor as kings under the Order of Melchizedek.

My first notable experience plundering the Trading Floor as a priest and a king happened in February of 2004. My brother called from a hospital in Fort Lauderdale, Florida, to tell me that my dad was in intensive care; he was very ill, and the doctors could not determine what was wrong with him. My brother is very strong and rarely cries or shows emotion, but I could hear fear in his voice and I knew this was very serious. I immediately booked my flight to Florida and then went into my prayer closet. I asked the Lord if I should prepare myself for my dad's departure. The Lord responded, "This sickness is not unto death, but for the glory of God." After arriving at the airport, I called my friend, Peggy, who prayed with me and prophesied that I was the "sent one." This prophetic word gave me peace and a sense of security, causing a new authority in God to arise within my spirit. When I arrived at the hospital, it was far worse than I had imagined; my dad was hooked up to more tubes and medical equipment than I had ever seen before. Even though he was unconscious, I sensed that he was in tremendous pain and agony. It seemed this was going to be quite a journey and, indeed, it was.

For the first three days, my dad did not even know I was there with him because he was totally unconscious. The Lord told me before I left for Florida, "This sickness is not unto death but for the Glory of God." The Lord said this same thing regarding Lazarus' illness, and on the fourth day the Lord raised him from the dead. I felt faith arise within me for that fourth day anointing. I said, "Lord, it has been three days and my dad doesn't even know that I am here. Surely, You love me as much as You loved Mary and Martha. I need to know You are with me on this journey." God is so merciful and faithful. The moment my foot crossed the threshold of my dad's hospital room on that fourth day He sat up in bed and said, "What are you doing here?" I was very excited that he sat up and acknowledged my presence. The excitement did not last long because within minutes he was unconscious again; however, I thanked God for the amazing sign on the fourth day!

Six more days passed and the doctors still did not know what was wrong. They gave us almost no hope saying there was nothing more they could do for him and he was too weak to fly to Boston for more specialized care. Throughout the entire ten days I had been pleading on my dad's behalf as a priest in the courts of Heaven. I repented for all his sins, my sins and the sins of our ancestors. I was not ready to lose my dad and I knew he was not right with the Lord. Even though he had said the sinner's prayer a few years before, he was doing a lot of illegal trading with the enemy and I knew it. The enemy came to stake his claim by taking my dad's life prematurely, just like he had Lazarus.

By the mercy of the Lord, the doctors decided to do exploratory surgery. They had tried to avoid doing the surgery, knowing it could result in tremendous poisons being released into Dad's system that could cause all his organs to shut down, actually resulting in death from the surgery itself. We were desperate, knowing he was going to die without it, so we asked the surgeon to go forward with the surgery. The doctors discovered an aneurism in my dad's intestine that caused a large portion of the intestine to turn gangrenous and die. They removed the dead portion and, indeed, his body went into shock due to the release of much poison into his system. The doctors gave us very little hope for his survival, as he was already so weak. Suddenly, the haunting sounds of a Code Blue reverberated throughout my dad's room, indicating that my dad was in grave danger. Doctors and nurses began rushing to my dad's side and began attempts to save him; he was dying. Even though the situation was intense I had peace and decided to find a place to pray.

I found a column of meal trays in the hallway of the intensive care unit and decided to duck behind them to intercede. I began to pray in the Holy Spirit with great intensity. I noticed that by the way I was positioning my right hand that I had an instrument of authority in it. I now know it was the ruling scepter that would not depart from Judah (Psalm 110). As I prayed in the Spirit I heard my voice rise many levels in authority and then all of a sudden my prayer tongues turned to English and I began to say, "Pass Over, Pass Over, Pass Over," in a strong, deep and authoritative voice. It was not long before my mind joined in with my spirit and I realized that the Holy Spirit was telling the angel of death to pass over my dad's room! I was so excited knowing that the Holy Spirit was warring on our behalf. I then said something like, "Yeah, you must pass over. The blood of Jesus makes atonement for my dad and it covers him, etc..." Then I began to decree like a king in battle. Because the blood had legally been applied with ten days of repentance, the courts were set to answer in our favor. All the repentance over the past ten days gave God the judicial right according to His own laws to rule in favor of extended life for my dad!

The next morning my dad was sitting up in his hospital bed totally awake. He recognized me as soon as I walked in. He wanted to have a meal with me, and that is when I knew my dad was back!

My precious dad lived to tell of the Lord's great mercy and because of his near-death experience he fully gave his life to the Lord and was water baptized a few weeks later. During the time my dad was so sick, I asked the Lord for fifteen extended years of life for him, remembering that Hezekiah asked the Lord for fifteen additional years to live. I did not know whether that petition would be granted, but exactly seven and one-half years later, my dad passed to Heaven from an aneurism in his heart. I guess the Lord's answer to me was that He would meet me half-way. My dad did not die in any pain or suffering and by the end of his life, he was praying every night on his knees by his bedside before he went to sleep. He and I had many conversations about the Lord and we loved to pray together often. My dad learned to love during the last seven and one-half years of his life, but most importantly he learned to love the One who saved him from death and hell in that hospital room on that eventful day! Thank God for the blood of Jesus!

I believe the same was the case when Lazarus was put in the grave prematurely. Jesus spent three days interceding for him as a priest. Once the priestly intercession was complete in the courts of Heaven Jesus showed up on the fourth day and called Lazarus forth as a King on the battlefield. We are kings and priests in the Order of Melchizedek and we are to rule and reign the same way Jesus did while He was on earth.

Argue Your Case, State Your Cause

Repentance is the only way to absolute victory. The blood of Jesus legally wipes away every sin, all iniquitous patterns and any illegal trade, but the blood must be applied! That is why in Isaiah 43 God also says, *"Put Me in remembrance; let us argue our case together, state your cause, that you may be proved right."* Jesus, our Advocate, is sitting at the right hand of the Righteous Judge waiting to make intercession for us with His blood. We just have to enter His courts and plead our case.

Acts of illegal trade become court cases in Heaven, just as illegal acts become court cases on earth. We have to deal with these issues as in a court.

194

**Righteous are You, O Lord, that I would plead
my case with You; indeed I would discuss
matters of justice with You…**

—Jeremiah 12:1

**"Present your case," the Lord says. "Bring
forward your strong arguments," the King of
Jacob says.**

—Isaiah 41:21

It is God's desire for us to come before Him as witnesses, bringing forth our cases of injustice to the Righteous Judge of the universe. Who may bring a charge against God's elect? It is God who justifies. God always desires to justify us. His answer is always, "Yes, I forgive you." He already forgave us when His Son Jesus shed His blood on the cross over 2,000 years ago. But just as the blood has to be applied for salvation, it also has to be applied for deliverance from the illegal trade schemes of the enemy. Simply put, we have to apply His blood in the courts of Heaven.

Agree with Your Opponent at Law

"You have heard that the ancients were told, 'You shall not commit murder' and 'Whoever commits murder shall be liable to the court.' But I say to you that everyone who is angry with **his brother shall be guilty before the court; and whoever says to his brother, 'You good-for-nothing,' shall be guilty before the supreme court;** and whoever says, 'You fool,' shall be guilty enough to go into the fiery hell."

—Matthew 5:21-22

This Scripture tells us that we can be held guilty before the court. Jesus advises us against being adversarial with our opponent at law (Satan, the accuser) on our way to court!

"Make friends quickly with your opponent at law while you are with him on the way, [to court] so that your opponent may not hand you over to the judge and the judge to the officer, and you be thrown into prison. Truly I say to you, you will not come out of there until you have paid up the last cent."

—Matthew 5:25-26

Satan, our accuser, takes us to court, launching accusations against us. Jesus advises us to agree with him on the way so that we won't be thrown in jail. What we must do is agree with his accusations against us and repent for them so we will be exonerated. The blood paid in full for every one of our sins and cancels every accusation against us! Accusations are the strong armor that the enemy trusts in. The Bible says that before we can plunder the enemy's house (Trading Floor located in the second heaven) we have to first take away his armor in which he trusts.

Take His Armor Away

"But if I cast out demons by the finger of God, then the kingdom of God has come upon you. **When a strong man, fully armed, guards his own house, his possessions are undisturbed. But when someone stronger than he attacks him and overpowers him, he takes away from him all his armor on which he had relied and distributes his plunder."**

—Luke 11:20-22

Satan's armor is his legal accusations against us for using Sin's Intellectual Property. He trusts in his legal claims and accusations. However, without them he has no case against us and he is easily plundered! Once we disarm him from his hostile decrees of accusation we can plunder his house and possessions, which are his Trading Floor and altars!

When you were dead in your transgressions
and the uncircumcision of your flesh, He made
you alive together with Him, **having forgiven
us all our transgressions, having canceled out
the certificate of debt consisting of decrees
against us, which was hostile to us; and He has
taken it out of the way, having nailed it to the
cross. When He had disarmed the rulers and
authorities, He made a public display of them,
having triumphed over them through Him.**
—Colossians 2:13-15

What About Job?

I truly believe that if Job would have agreed with his adversary on the way to court he could have saved himself and his family a whole lot of pain. Let's look at a few points in the story of Job.

First of all, we see that the setting is a courtroom:

**One day the members of the heavenly court
came to present themselves before the Lord,
and the Accuser, Satan, came with them.**
—Job 1:6 NLT

For some reason the Lord asked Satan if he had considered His righteous servant Job. I believe the reason the Lord wanted Satan to consider Job is because he was indeed the Lord's faithful servant, but there was something in his life that God wanted to address. The process of "the threshing floor" begins for Job. The Lord gave Satan permission to sift him (Job 1:12).

Job goes through tremendous loss: All his possessions are wiped out, his ten children die and then he is badly afflicted with boils all over his body. Job says, **"What I always feared has happened to me. What I dreaded has come true"** (Job 3:25, NLT).

Here we see a couple of issues that God wants to deal with in Job's life. It is not God's will for us to live in fear and dread. Even more importantly, Job did not completely trust God, so there was a heart issue present, as well. In addition, Job could have very well been trading with words of fear and dread through his mouth gate!

God has not given us a spirit of fear, but of love, power and a sound mind. The spirit of fear and dread comes from the domain of darkness. God wanted Job to be delivered from fear, as it is a demonic technology that brings torment. I believe Job tapped into the technology of fear on a regular basis and God's father heart wanted to deliver him. God's desire was for Job to trust in Him completely and to live in perfect peace.

> **"The steadfast of mind You will keep in perfect peace, because he trusts in You."**
> —Isaiah 26:3

From the very beginning of the story, God had Job's best interest at heart because He loved His servant Job deeply.

The other issue I noticed with Job is that he insisted he was blameless before God (Job 9:21; 31:6). Job chose not to agree with the accuser on the way to court. Satan, the accuser, used Job's three friends as the accusers, but instead of searching his heart to see if at least some of what they said may be true, he chose to stand strong in his position as "I am blameless before God." Job did not believe he had any reason to repent.

Scripture says that ALL have sinned and have fallen short of the glory of God; that means ALL, even Job. The Scripture also tells us that of ALL of the sons of men, not just the nation of Israel, but out of ALL the sons of men, not one understands and there is not one who does good (Psalms 14 and 53). The Apostle Paul quotes this in Romans 3:9-18.

Job recites all his righteous acts before God (Job 29:12-17). Can we say that maybe, just maybe, Job had an issue with righteousness according to works and not faith?

God wanted to deepen Job's relationship with Him. He wanted Job to trust Him completely. There is no righteousness outside of relationship and trust in God.

As a matter of fact, the only righteousness that impresses God is the righteous act of His Son Jesus Christ on the cross. God is pleased with those who enter by faith into the work of Calvary and not by their own works. Jesus imputed His righteousness to us as a free gift!

> He made Him who knew no sin to be sin on our behalf, so **that we might become the righteousness of God in Him.**
> —2 Corinthians 5:21

We are justified by faith, not our works. Job was testifying about His works, not his right standing with God through a relationship established in love and faith. God wanted to make a shift in Job's life.

Job knew he needed a mediator to go before him (Job 9:32-35) and he was correct in saying so. God Himself came to Job to intercept the destruction from going any further. Job listened to God and repented, and as soon as he repented, his captivity was turned! Then Job prayed for his friends and he ended up with TWICE as much as he had before he was taken to court by the adversary! Job plundered the Trading Floor with repentance for himself (Job 42:6) and prayer for his friends!

There was glory at the end of the threshing floor for Job!

Agreeing with our adversary by repenting and applying the blood of Jesus is the only way to plunder the enemy's Trading Floor.

In some court cases we have to be very specific in our repentance, as was the case for my husband and me when we found ourselves in a very hard place.

A Very Hard Place

The Lord's blessings really began to manifest in our lives around 2006. My husband and I felt like it was a great time for us to invest in real estate. We bought a couple of houses and four acres of land in addition to our own home. As you know, the real estate market took a huge hit in the Phoenix area beginning in about the year 2008. By that time we had already invested in the properties. We had a note on the land and, unfortunately, we were unable to sell it for anywhere near the amount at which we purchased it. My bright idea was to take out a second mortgage against our residence for the land, so the payments would be lower and we could write off the interest on our taxes. (You can't write off interest on land loans.) We qualified for the line of credit against our home, but the only problem was the market tanked even more and we ended up very "upside down" in our own home!

My husband and I had very good credit and lived within our means. We were totally against debt unless it was for an investment property. We basically lived debt-free outside of these so-called real estate investments. We had worked very hard to build the equity in our home and to stay out of debt. Our intention was to flip the properties and move on to new investments, but things did not work out as we planned!

The fact that we were financially upside down in our home began to weigh very heavily on us and we knew God had to have a solution. We didn't believe we were to short sell our home because we didn't sense the time had come for us to move. I began to seek the Lord regarding what to do about the dilemma. He reminded me of something that occurred about eleven years before. We built a pool and acted as the general contractor; one of the subcontractors never billed us for his services. I believe I tried to contact him, but I never pursued paying him when he didn't respond to the phone call. At the time, we thought that it was a blessing from the Lord and that the guy decided not to charge us.

We were dead wrong; it was not a blessing from the Lord but a set up from the enemy. Satan totally deceived us. Remember, deception is the stock and trade of his kingdom. My husband and I would never intentionally cheat or steal from anyone, in fact, we give lots of money away! What we thought was a blessing was actually a set up for a curse! We were supposed to keep pursuing the subcontractor until we found him and paid him for his services!

Fast forward, here we are eleven years later and the Lord reminds me that we never paid that contractor. Even though he never billed us or responded when we called him, we should have pursued paying him as that would have been the righteous thing to do. But instead, we thought the blessing of "no bill" was from the Lord. See how the enemy deceived us? This was a demonic trade and we fell right into it unknowingly.

When the Lord reminded me of this instance I immediately called my husband. He could not recall the situation as it really wasn't a big deal to us at the time, since we did not know we were trading! I am being very transparent here because I want you to understand how deceptive the enemy is in getting us to trade, and how sometimes we need to be very specific in our repentance. We need to go to the throne room and hear with our spiritual ears what accusations are standing against us. There may be several, and there could also be accusations against our bloodline. He who has an ear to hear, let him hear what the Spirit says (Revelation 2:17).

I told my husband that we needed to specifically repent for that one sin and apply the blood of Jesus, and we did. At about the same time, we gave a very significant offering to the Lord not knowing that it would act as a peace offering for us. Now the Lord was setting us up to plunder the enemy's Trading Floor!

Sometimes it may take more than just repentance. God may require other righteous acts to make things right in order to turn the Trading Floors in our favor. In our case, we had no idea who the subcontractor was because the incident occurred many years before; there was no way to make it right with him. I believe the Lord required a peace offering from us instead. It just so happened that as we were repenting for this sin, we felt led to give the Lord a very large offering which was over and above our tithe. The Lord later revealed to me that it was a peace offering.

Remember, David stayed the plague against Israel with repentance and a peace offering. The peace offering was used when someone was in desperate need of deliverance. If a man was in need of mercy he would add a peace offering to his prayer. The peace offering was not part of the Mosaic Law, so it still applies to us today. The peace offering is a freewill offering of love and gratitude.

Very shortly afterwards, during my prayer time the Lord gave me the strategy of how to plunder the enemy's Trading Floor. I called the bank and told them that we wanted to short sell our house to ourselves. Believe it or not, they agreed! We paid the amount they required to pay off our second mortgage and the result was debt cancellation of well over $100,000! That was not the only blessing; we were able to legally keep the four acres of land, and overnight we had ALL the equity in our home restored! The second mortgage payment was dissolved, all the equity was restored and the four acres of land was ours to keep free and clear!

The Lord showed me that it was that one single "not so innocent" trade with darkness that caused us all the loss in the real estate market.

Remember, the children of the world can use Sin's technology all they want, but we, the children of light, cannot use it or Satan will exact wages from us for using Sin's Intellectual Property.

The enemy knows our weaknesses and tries very hard to capitalize on them, just like when he went to Jesus in His weak moment of hunger after forty days of fasting. It was a weak moment for us because we were tight on cash, we had just bought a new home, and we were building a pool and putting in landscaping. We have to be very aware of his trade schemes! Be on the alert, the devil, your adversary, prowls around seeking someone to devour!

But once the accuser is cast down the power and glory of our God comes!

> Then I heard a loud voice in heaven, saying, **"Now the salvation, and the power, and the kingdom of our God and the authority of His Christ have come, for the accuser of our brethren has been thrown down, he who accuses them before our God day and night."**
>
> —Revelation 12:10

Righteous Trading

Here is a personal testimony when righteous trading is in place: In 1995 my previous husband left our family for another lifestyle outside of our Christian family life. We were devastated to say the least. I looked at our lives and all the pain we were going through and thought to myself, "This can't be right, this can't be right. I am not reaping what I've sown; this just can't be my harvest." The divorce was very, very intense. My then ten-year-old son Joshua was dismissed from nine schools that year because of the hurt and anger regarding losing his dad. I had to sit in front of nine principals and hear how deeply traumatized my son was and how he could not function in a normal school setting. At the time, I had to work full-time because there was no child support. How was I to home-school Joshua and work to support us? Joshua ended up at a boy's ranch because there was just no other alternative, and that alone pained us greatly.

The trauma went on and on. I will spare you the rest of the details, but the enemy's plan was to destroy us emotionally and mentally. I brought forth my strong arguments before the Lord and stated my cause. I told the Lord that this could not be my harvest. "This is not what I get," I said. "This is illegal activity on the part of the enemy because I did not sow for this harvest." Although divorce was strong on my side of the family I had repented for it, prayed against it and prayed for God's blessing on our marriage and family. So I brought my case before God. I told Him that I rejected the harvest I was receiving. The Lord asked me what I wanted. I told Him that I knew what I did not want and that was to be a single mom working two and three jobs to try to support my emotionally damaged children. Then I told Him what I did want, which was to be married to a good responsible Christian man who would love my children as his own. I wanted my family restored! At that time I was about half-way through a forty-day fast for my marriage and family. The Lord released me from the fast and I knew He was also releasing me from the marriage. I sat my two children down and told them that I was planning to file for divorce. I told them that I would remarry someday, but I would make sure that I married a man that would love them and honor them. They agreed with the plan!

The following week I went to an attorney's office to file for divorce and I met Andrew Coventry, my present husband of over seventeen years! He was the paralegal that was assigned to my "court case." Of course we did not start to date right away, and I had no idea he would soon become my husband. Andy had just broken off a long-term relationship and he arrived at the attorney's office in July of 1995, the same month that I did. His degree was in sales and marketing, but he was considering furthering his degree to become an attorney at law. I truly believe the Lord gave him that idea so he could meet me! He eventually realized that he did not like the law field and went back to his career in sales and marketing soon after we were married.

When Andy and I met, his salary was low because he was a new paralegal. I told the Lord that I had forgotten to put "abundant provider" down on my list. The Lord assured me that if I married this man He would bless him as my husband. The rest of our story is His Story of love and faithfulness, but, most of all, of justice. My marriage to Andy is the marriage that I had been praying for all those years. The altar on the Trading Floor of Heaven was filled with my prayers. As I brought forth my strong arguments before the courts of Heaven, the courts responded in my favor because the blood had already been applied many times and many years in advance.

Mercy Triumphed

God is no respecter of persons. He is our Righteous Judge. Most times we approach Him as our loving Father, our Abba, and we just sit at His feet to commune and worship Him. I love those moments; most of the time that is how I am positioned before Him. However, there are times in our lives when we must approach Him as the Righteous Judge. His throne is a throne of mercy and His desire is to always rule in favor of justice!

In the courts of Heaven, mercy triumphs over judgment. God's mercy triumphed in all of our lives. I married the man of my dreams and my children received an amazing stepdad. They, as well as our grandchildren, absolutely adore Andy. My former husband was restored to his children a few years after the divorce was final. When our daughter, Jennah, was married both her biological dad and her stepdad walked her down the aisle. God blessed Joshua with a son of his own, he has become a loving and devoted father. What a picture of restoration and healing. God's mercies are new every morning and great is His faithfulness!

God has positioned Himself on the Mercy Seat and He is ready to rule in your favor!

LIFE APPLICATION SECTION

Memory Verse:

Then I heard a loud voice in heaven, saying, "Now the salvation, and the power, and the kingdom of our God and the authority of His Christ have come, for the accuser of our brethren has been thrown down, he who accuses them before our God day and night."

—Revelation 12:10

Reflections:

What should we do while on our way to court with our opponent at law?

_____

_____

_____

What was Job's mistake?

_____

_____

_____

What weapons do we use to plunder the enemy's Trading Floor?

_____

_____

_____

JOURNAL YOUR THOUGHTS

_____

_____

_____

_____

_____

_____

_____

_____

_____

_____

_____

_____

_____

_____

_____

_____

_____

_____

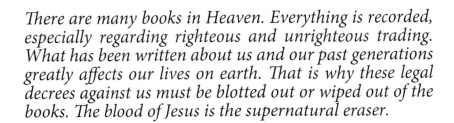

There are many books in Heaven. Everything is recorded, especially regarding righteous and unrighteous trading. What has been written about us and our past generations greatly affects our lives on earth. That is why these legal decrees against us must be blotted out or wiped out of the books. The blood of Jesus is the supernatural eraser.

11

MAKE GAINS BY TRADING

One evening as I was preparing a message, the Lord led me to the Scripture where Jesus is talking to His followers about loaves of bread.

> Jesus answered them and said, "Truly, truly, I say
> to you, you seek Me, not because you saw signs,
> but because you ate of the loaves and were filled.
> Do not work for the food which perishes, but
> for the food which endures to eternal life, which
> the Son of Man will give to you, for on Him the
> Father, God, has set His seal."
>
> —John 6:26-27

The Word Elevates

The root word for *loaves* is *airo* which means "to raise upwards, to elevate, to raise from the ground, to lift up." Jesus, the Word of God, is the Bread that came down from Heaven. Revelation of Him lifts us up in stature and positions us in a place to prevail in life.

> **"I am the living bread that came down out of heaven;** if anyone eats of this bread, he will live forever; and the bread also which I will give for the life of the world is My flesh."
>
> —John 6:51

> "He who eats My flesh and drinks My blood has eternal life, and I will **raise him up on the last day.**"
>
> —John 6:54

Revelation Brings Elevation

When we feed on Jesus, the Word of God, the Holy Spirit brings revelation, and revelation brings elevation.

The revelation of God's Word brought elevation to Noah and his family on the "last day of life on earth" for man and beast. Every living thing, except Noah and his family and two of every kind of animal, was destroyed in the great flood. Noah received the Word that God gave him when God told him to build an ark. He ate the Living Word. The word elevated the ark and his family above destruction in the day of judgment.

Let's look again at the focal passage of Scripture for this chapter:

> Jesus answered them and said, "Truly, truly, I say to you, you seek Me, not because you saw signs,

but because you ate of the loaves and were filled.
**Do not work for the food which perishes, but
for the food which endures to eternal life,** which
the Son of Man will give to you, for on Him the
Father, God, has set His seal."

—John 6:26-27

The Greek transliteration for the word *work* is *ergazomai*
which means to **make gains by trading or doing business**! We
can make gains that will endure to eternal life by trading our life
for the Word of God. Being about our Father's business is the way
to make gains that will endure through eternity. God's business is
building His Kingdom on earth with His Word, Jesus.

Listen, Receive and Obey

Noah listened to the Word of God, received the Word of God
and obeyed the Word of God. This brought him and his family
great dividends in trade.

Then God said to Noah, "The end of all flesh
has come before Me; for the earth is filled with
violence because of them; and behold, I am about
to destroy them with the earth. **Make for yourself
an ark of gopher wood;** you shall make the ark
with rooms, and shall cover it inside and out with
pitch."

—Genesis 6:13-14

Noah's trade was hearing the Word (even though Genesis
wasn't the written Word yet), receiving the Word, and obeying
the Word. His reward was salvation for his entire family. As hard
as it was to obey, he obeyed. That's where the trade was transacted.
Noah made gains for himself and his family by trading obedience
to the Word of God. Noah chose obedience to the Word instead of
all the other things he could have chosen to do with his life during

that time period. He traded his life, time, talents, and resources to obey the Word of God. The trade lifted and elevated him and his family in the day of destruction.

Noah had a revelation from God regarding what was coming to the earth and what to do to escape. Obeying the revelation brought elevation to him and his family in the time of great disaster! Revelation always brings elevation. We can make gains by trading for the Word, the Bread of Life, which will elevate and lift us up over natural circumstances no matter how difficult they may be.

Prevail through Revelation

In Scripture water is often symbolic of revelation from the Holy Spirit. Revelation is received by the Holy Spirit from the Word of God. In the next Scripture reference notice that it was the water that prevailed in the day of Noah.

> **Then the flood came upon the earth for forty days, and the water increased and lifted up the ark, so that it rose above the earth. The water prevailed and increased greatly upon the earth, and the ark floated on the surface of the water. The water prevailed more and more upon the earth, so that all the high mountains everywhere under the heavens were covered. The water prevailed fifteen cubits higher, and the mountains were covered. All flesh that moved on the earth perished,** birds and cattle and beasts and every swarming thing that swarms upon the earth, and all mankind; of all that was on the dry land, all in whose nostrils was the breath of the spirit of life, died. Thus He blotted out every living thing that was upon the face of the land, from

man to animals to creeping things and to birds of the sky, and they were blotted out from the earth; **and only Noah was left, together with those that were with him in the ark.**

—Genesis 7:17-23

Revelation from the Holy Spirit regarding the Word that Noah received caused the ark that he and his family entered to be lifted up. The ark was raised above all the destruction that came upon the earth. The revelation that came to Noah by the Holy Spirit (symbolized by the water) caused Noah and his family to be lifted above the high mountains. It caused all flesh that was not in agreement with the revelation of the Word to die.

In Scripture many times mountains symbolize government. When we invest our lives in the Word and receive revelation concerning the Word, even the governments of this world will be beneath us because we will be elevated to higher places by the Spirit of God. We will always know what to do to prevail even in the most difficult of times.

God released a prevailing word of revelation to Zerubbabel, the governor of Judah during a challenging time in his nation.

Then he said to me, "This is the word of the Lord to Zerubbabel saying, **'Not by might nor by power, but by My Spirit,'** says the Lord of hosts. **'What are you, O great mountain? Before Zerubbabel you will become a plain; and he will bring forth the top stone with shouts of "Grace, grace to it!"'**"

—Zechariah 4:6-7

Revelation Brings Death to Flesh

When the water prevailed during the flood all flesh died. Revelation from the Word of God will cause our flesh to die. The flesh sets itself against the spirit. Death to the flesh means life in the Spirit. Life in the Spirit will cause us to prevail over all natural circumstances.

God is showing us that we should make gains in life by trading our lives for the Word of God like Noah did. In doing so, revelation from the Word will lift us up above death and destruction, should it come our way. It will give us the power to prevail even in the darkest days. Jesus said that the days of Noah would manifest on earth again.

> **"And just as it happened in the days of Noah, so it will be also in the days of the Son of Man:** they were eating, they were drinking, they were marrying, they were being given in marriage, until the day that Noah entered the ark, and the flood came and destroyed them all."
>
> —Luke 17:26-27

Quick Review

We will prevail in life through revelation from the Holy Spirit regarding the Word of God, which is the Bread of Life that elevates us. The Word of God, the bread, elevates us and the water, the revelation from the Word, causes us to prevail!

Jesus Offers Living Water

> Jesus answered and said to her "If you knew the gift of God, and who it is who says to you, 'Give Me a drink,' you would have asked Him, **and He would have given you living water."**
>
> —John 4:10

> Now on the last day, the great day of the feast, Jesus stood and cried out, saying, "If anyone is thirsty, let him come to Me and drink. He who

believes in Me, as the Scripture said, **'From his innermost being will flow rivers of living water.'"**

—John 7:37-38

When we release the Word into the lives of others or over our own lives, revelation comes and it causes those who hear to prevail in life. Just as Noah and his family prevailed, we shall also prevail in these final days before Jesus returns.

His Voice Is Like Water

God speaks through us. We have His voice upon the waters within us.

His feet were like burnished bronze, when it has been made to glow in a furnace, **and His voice was like the sound of many waters.**

—Revelation 1:15

The voice of the Lord is upon the waters; the God of glory thunders, **the Lord is over many waters.**

—Psalm 29:3

The voice of the Lord is upon the waters and the water of God's Spirit is now in us! He promised that He would not flood the earth again with natural water but that the knowledge of His glory would cover the earth as the waters cover the sea. The knowledge of His glory (revelation) will be released through His Spirit within us.

"For the earth will be filled with the knowledge of the glory of the Lord, as the waters cover the sea."

—Habakkuk 2:14

God Performs His Word

I feel really fortunate that early in my walk with the Lord I learned the importance of knowing God's Word. I was taught that not only was it important to receive God's Word implanted (James 1:21), but it was also important to speak the Word of God out loud, because faith comes by hearing and hearing by the Word of God.

From the book of Genesis I learned that the Spirit of the Lord would hover and wait for the Word to be spoken so that He could create with it.

> In the beginning God created the heavens and the earth. Now the earth was formless and empty, darkness was over the surface of the deep, **and the Spirit of God was hovering over the waters. And God said, "Let there be light," and there was light.**
> —Genesis 1:1-3 NIV

Jeremiah tells us that God looks for His word to perform it.

> Then the Lord said to me, "You have seen well, **for I am watching over My word to perform it."**
> —Jeremiah 1:12

Ezekiel states that God speaks His word and performs it.

> **"For I the Lord will speak, and whatever word I speak will be performed.** It will no longer be delayed, for in your days, O rebellious house, **I will speak the word and perform it,"** declares the Lord God.
> —Ezekiel 12:25

God Confirms His Word

Isaiah tells us that God confirms the word of His servant and performs the purpose of His messengers.

> "**Confirming the word of His servant** and performing the purpose of His messengers."
> —Isaiah 44:26

God also says that His word will not return empty, but will accomplish what God desires and it will succeed in the matter for which it is sent.

> "**So will My word be which goes forth from My mouth; It will not return to Me empty, without accomplishing what I desire, and without succeeding in the matter for which I sent it.**"
> —Isaiah 55:11

Another reason why it is important to pray the Word of God out loud is because when the angels hear it they perform it. The angels will obey the voice of our commands if our commands agree with the Word of God.

> **Bless the Lord, you His angels, mighty in strength, who perform His word, obeying the voice of His word!** Bless the Lord, all you His hosts, you who serve Him, doing His will.
> —Psalm 103:20-21

God Magnifies His Word above His Name

> I will worship toward Your holy temple and praise Your name for Your loving kindness and for Your truth and faithfulness; for You have exalted above

all else Your name and Your word and **You have magnified Your word above all Your name.**
—Psalm 138:2 AMP

God's Word Will Never Pass Away

The books of Matthew, Mark and Luke all state that Heaven and earth will pass away but God's Word will never, ever pass away.

Heaven and earth will pass away, **but My words will not pass away.**
—Matthew 24:35

God's Word will never pass away because Jesus is God's Word. Jesus will never pass away. He is the Beginning and the End, the First and the Last, the Alpha and Omega, the Eternal Father, the Everlasting God!

Nothing in life has any value in comparison to the Word of God because it is all passing away. Only what we invest in or trade for through the Word of God will remain forever.

But the day of the Lord will come like a thief, **in which the heavens will pass away with a roar and the elements will be destroyed with intense heat, and the earth and its works will be burned up.**
—2 Peter 3:10

Trading Our Resources

Many times when I receive an offering I tell those listening to trade their natural finances for the Word of promise that I am releasing at the time. We can make gains by trading or investing our finances in God's Word. Natural wealth has no eternal value.

Only what we do with our wealth has lasting value. We can make gains by trading our finances for God's Eternal Word.

There are many ways we can make gains by trading in God's Kingdom. Any time we invest our finances, our time, our service or talents into the Word of God for advancement in His Kingdom we are making gains by trading in our Father's business.

Jesus Is the Word

> In the beginning was the Word, and the Word was with God, and the **Word was God.**
>
> —John 1:1

When the final battle comes it will be Jesus, the Word of God, who prevails over the wickedness of the nations.

> And I saw heaven opened, and behold, a white horse, and He who sat on it is called Faithful and True, and in righteousness He judges and wages war. His eyes are a flame of fire, and on His head are many diadems; and He has a name written on Him which no one knows except Himself. **He is clothed with a robe dipped in blood, and His name is called The Word of God.** And the armies which are in heaven, clothed in fine linen, white and clean, were following Him on white horses. From His mouth comes a sharp sword, so that with it He may strike down the nations, and He will rule them with a rod of iron; and He treads the wine press of the fierce wrath of God, the Almighty. And on His robe and on His thigh He has a name written, **"KING OF KINGS, AND LORD OF LORDS."**
>
> —Revelation 19:11-16

Only One Worthy

Let's look at the focal passage of Scripture for this chapter one last time:

> Jesus answered them and said, "Truly, truly, I say
> to you, you seek Me, not because you saw signs,
> but because you ate of the loaves and were filled.
> Do not work for the food which perishes, but
> for the food which endures to eternal life, which
> the Son of Man will give to you, **for on Him the
> Father, God, has set His seal."**
> —John 6:26-27

God has set His seal on Jesus, the Word of God. The Word is a sure investment and it will always bring great dividends to our heavenly bank accounts. Not only has God the Father set His seal on Jesus, but Jesus is the only ONE WORTHY to break the seals of the books in Heaven.

> **"Worthy are You to take the book and to break
> its seals;** for You were slain, and purchased for
> God with Your blood men from every tribe and
> tongue and people and nation. You have made
> them to be a kingdom and priests to our God; and
> they will reign upon the earth."
> Then I looked, and I heard the voice of many
> angels around the throne and the living
> creatures and the elders; and the number of
> them was myriads of myriads, and thousands of
> thousands, saying with a loud voice,
> **"Worthy is the Lamb** that was slain to receive power
> and riches and wisdom and might and honor and
> glory and blessing."
> And every created thing which is in heaven and on
> the earth and under the earth and on the sea, and all

things in them, I heard saying,

**"To Him who sits on the throne, and to the Lamb,
be blessing and honor and glory and dominion
forever and ever."**
And the four living creatures kept saying, "Amen."
And the elders fell down and worshiped.

—Revelation 5:9-14

Only Jesus, the Word of God is worthy. He is the only One worth trading for the things we value in this life. Jesus, the Word of God, the Bread of Life, is the Pearl of Great Price!

"Again, the kingdom of heaven is like a merchant
seeking fine pearls, and upon finding ONE PEARL
of great value, **he went and sold all that he had
and bought it."**

—Matthew 13:45-46

"The kingdom of heaven is like a treasure hidden
in the field, which a man found and hid again; **and
from joy over it he goes and sells all that he has
and buys that field."**

—Matthew 13:44

It's time to SELL OUT for Jesus, the Word of God! This is how we make great gains by trading!

LIFE APPLICATION SECTION

Memory Verse:

Jesus answered them and said, "Truly, truly, I say to you, you seek Me, not because you saw signs, but because you ate of the loaves and were filled. Do not work for the food which perishes, but for the food which endures to eternal life, which the Son of Man will give to you, for on Him the Father, God, has set His seal."

—John 6:26-27

Reflections:

What does the root word for loaves, *airo,* mean?

_____

_____

_____

What does the word *work* in the above Scripture actually mean in Greek?

_____

_____

_____

How do we make gains by trading in God's Kingdom?

_____

_____

_____

JOURNAL YOUR THOUGHTS

_____

_____

_____

_____

_____

_____

_____

_____

_____

_____

_____

_____

_____

_____

_____

_____

_____

_____

_____

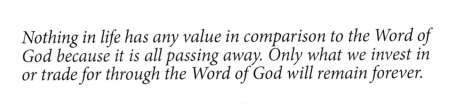

Nothing in life has any value in comparison to the Word of God because it is all passing away. Only what we invest in or trade for through the Word of God will remain forever.

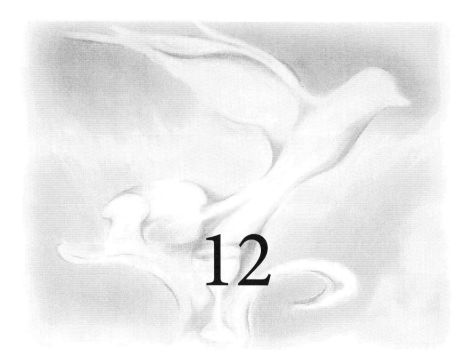

TRADE WINDS FROM HEAVEN

God's wisdom is revealed in nature. We can receive much revelation about our Creator and how He operates within the Kingdom of God by looking to His creation on earth. Jesus used nature many times to teach the disciples important truths about the Kingdom.

One example is the parable about the sower as recorded in Mark 4. Jesus used the illustration of planting seed in natural ground to teach a very important spiritual truth regarding sowing and reaping. As a matter of fact, He told the disciples that if they didn't understand this one important parable they would not be able understand all the other parables.

One day the Lord impressed upon me that He wanted to teach me about spiritual trade winds. He encouraged me to learn about natural trade winds first. I was reminded of a Scripture in First Corinthians:

> However, **the spiritual is not first, but the natural;** then the spiritual.
> —1 Corinthians 15:46

Natural Trade Winds

Trade winds were named for their ability to quickly propel trading ships across the ocean. The term *trade* was originally derived from a Middle English word meaning track or path rather than commerce. The winds would create a track or path that blew the trading ships across the ocean quickly.

Trade winds would help speed sailing. It was important to stay with the trade winds; otherwise, the ship could get stranded for long periods of time with no wind at all, risking the possibility of running out of supplies.

As early as the fifteenth century the Portuguese recognized the importance of trade winds to navigating in the Atlantic Ocean. The captain of a sail ship would seek a course along which the winds could be expected to blow in the direction of anticipated sailing. Prevailing winds made various points of the globe easy or difficult to access.

Trade winds create precipitation. Precipitation occurs when a local portion of the atmosphere becomes saturated with water vapor.

Trade winds are important because they bring a change of season! They shift the atmosphere![1]

Spiritual Trade Winds

Trade winds are the fast lane to getting a ship loaded with cargo to harbor! Is anyone waiting for their cargo-laden ship to come into port?

If so, then you will need heavenly trade winds to blow over the altars you have built to the Lord on the Trading Floor of Heaven. You might say, "What do trade winds have to do with Trading Floors?" I was hoping you would ask!

In the natural, trade winds blow over the seas to help propel the ship toward harbor quickly, with necessary trade of every kind. In the spirit we build altars on the Trading Floor of Heaven. The Trading Floor of Heaven is actually a sea of glass!

> **And before the throne there was something like a sea of glass,** like crystal; and in the center and around the throne, four living creatures full of eyes in front and behind.
> —Revelation 4:6

> **And I saw something like a sea of glass mixed with fire.**
> —Revelation 15:2

As we build altars of sacrifice, love and worship to the Lord on the sea of glass in Heaven, He consumes it with His fire. I believe that is why John saw a crystal sea of glass mixed with fire. When it is time for our harvest "ship" to come in with the goods we have been trading for, God causes trade winds to blow over the altars we have built on His Trading Floor, the sea of glass.

> When He utters His voice, **there is a tumult of waters in the heavens, and He causes the clouds to ascend from the end of the earth; He makes lightning for the rain, and brings out the WIND from His storehouses.**
> —Jeremiah 10:13 (Emphasis added)

The definition for *storehouses* is "treasure, gold, silver, store supplies, or treasury."

Whatever the Lord pleases, He does, in heaven and in earth, in the seas and in all deeps. He causes the vapors to ascend from the ends of the earth; who makes lightnings for the rain, **who brings forth the WIND from His TREASURIES.**
—Psalm 135:6-7 (Emphasis added)

Fire and hail, snow and clouds, **stormy wind, fulfilling His word.**
—Psalm 148:8

And of the angels He says, **"Who makes His angels winds,** and His ministers a flame of fire."
—Hebrews 1:7

Prevailing Winds

Not only do trade winds create a track or path to quickly bring trade in, they can also prevail to make certain points difficult to reach! When the trade winds begin to blow over the altars we have built to the Lord on the sea of glass, the Lord also sends His prevailing winds to thwart our adversaries, defending us and protecting our harvest! Pray that the Lord of Hosts will send His prevailing winds against your adversaries!

Let them be like **chaff before the wind,** with the angel of the Lord driving them on.
—Psalm 35:5

"You blew with Your wind, the sea covered them; they sank like lead in the mighty waters."
—Exodus 15:10

You contended with them by banishing them, by driving them away. **With His fierce wind He has expelled them** on the day of the east wind.
—Isaiah 27:8

Also note that if the trade winds don't blow, it causes the journey to come to a standstill in the middle of the sea. This creates times where we experience a sense of fruitlessness in our lives. It is vital to have the wind of God blowing in our favor or everything can get stuck on the sea of glass! Ask God to send His trade winds from Heaven to propel your ship toward its desired destination!

Water Vapor

Trade winds also create precipitation. Precipitation occurs when a local portion of the atmosphere becomes saturated with water vapor.

> **He causes the VAPORS to ascend from the ends**
> **of the earth; who makes lightnings for the rain,**
> **Who brings forth the WIND** from His treasuries.
> —Psalm 135:7 (Emphasis added)

Water vapor is necessary to cause the things we have planted in the spirit realm to grow. Trade winds will bring us from a dry season into a season of moisture and rain! Trade winds bring the rain of God! The rain of God brings great fruitfulness and harvest!

Ask Him

We have been given jurisdiction over the earth. The Lord wants us to ask Him to send His trade winds that will bring the rain. Wind from Heaven is a powerful force and God is ready to send it if we ask Him! He does nothing without revealing it to His servants the prophets, and He does nothing without our asking because the earth belongs to us.

> Surely the Lord God does **nothing unless He**
> **reveals His secret counsel to His servants the**
> **prophets.**
> —Amos 3:7

The heavens are the heavens of the Lord, **but the earth He has given to the sons of men.**

—Psalm 115:16

God is looking for His sons and daughters to partner with Him to make His dream for earth a reality. He wants the atmosphere of Heaven on earth. Jesus taught His disciples to pray, *"Our Father who is in Heaven, hallowed be Your name. **Your Kingdom come. Your will be done, on earth as it is in heaven.**"* The Kingdom of God manifesting on earth is His desire.

"Fear not, little flock; for it is your Father's good pleasure to give you the kingdom."

—Luke 12:32

"Until now you have asked for nothing in My name; **ask and you will receive, so that your joy may be made full.**"

—John 16:24

When our joy is full, His joy is full! He wants to give you His Kingdom! Most of all, He wants to give you His joy!

LIFE APPLICATION SECTION

Memory Verse:

When He utters His voice, there is a tumult of waters in the heavens, and He causes the clouds to ascend from the end of the earth; He makes lightning for the rain, and brings out the wind from His storehouses.

—Jeremiah 10:13

Reflections:

How do trade winds affect cargo ships?

_____

_____

_____

How do trade winds affect the atmosphere?

_____

_____

_____

What is the Trading Floor of Heaven?

_____

_____

_____

The Trading Floors

JOURNAL YOUR THOUGHTS

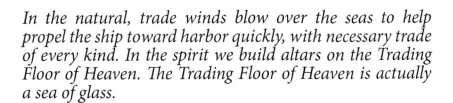

In the natural, trade winds blow over the seas to help propel the ship toward harbor quickly, with necessary trade of every kind. In the spirit we build altars on the Trading Floor of Heaven. The Trading Floor of Heaven is actually a sea of glass.

Epilogue

I would like to begin this Epilogue with the last Scripture mentioned in Chapter 12.

> "Until now you have asked for nothing in My name; ask and you will receive, **so that your joy may be made full.**"
>
> —John 16:24

Fullness of Joy

Several topics mentioned in this book are sobering, and many are about the importance of repentance. I believe it is a timely message for the Church, which is at the crossroads to her final point of destiny.

However, repentance is a place we visit when necessary. We do not live there forever! *The Kingdom of God is righteousness, peace and JOY in the Holy Spirit* (Romans 14:17)! Repentance is the way to salvation so we can live a life of great joy in His Presence. When the angel showed up to tell the shepherds of the birth of Jesus he said,

> "Do not be afraid for behold, I bring you **good news of great joy which will be for all the people;** for today in the city of David there has been born for you a Savior, who is Christ the Lord."
> —Luke 2:10

Although repentance is the first step to salvation from our enemies, it is also the first step to moving on to a life full of GREAT JOY and celebration because of what Jesus has done for all people!

> Then Nehemiah, who was the governor, and Ezra the priest and scribe, and the Levites who taught the people said to all the people, "This day is holy to the Lord your God; do not mourn or weep." For all the people were weeping when they heard the words of the law. Then he said to them, "Go, eat of the fat, drink of the sweet, and send portions to him who has nothing prepared; for this day is holy to our Lord. **Do not be grieved, for the joy of the Lord is your strength."**
> —Nehemiah 8:9-10

Nehemiah was the governor who brought the whole nation to repentance and rebuilt the wall around Jerusalem in fifty-two days. There was a time for repentance, but GREAT JOY was to be the result of their repentance, not sorrow!

Trade Sorrow for Joy

We can trade sorrow for joy! Remember it is a choice; we get to choose! Joy is technology from our Father in Heaven! Joy builds an altar of worship to the Lord, especially when we choose joy at a time when all hell is breaking loose around us. That becomes a powerful trade!

Joy, gladness and praise are technologies from the Tree of Life and they attract life! Sadness, hopelessness, and grief are technologies from the Tree of the Knowledge of Good and Evil and they attract death! The "law of attraction" is a real spiritual law, so we must be aware of what we are resonating with in the spirit.

Depression has a frequency and it attracts similar forces. Joy has a frequency and it attracts like forces, as well! That is why it is so important to trade sorrow for joy even when everything is screaming "be sad." Resist the sadness and choose joy! Submit to God, resist the devil and he will flee (James 4:7)! Joy attracts the resources in God's Kingdom because the Kingdom of God is righteousness, peace and joy (Romans 14:17)!

One day I woke up feeling sad. A couple of things still had not turned out the way I had hoped. I was getting weary in well-doing and I just felt like being sad that day. I really did not plan on fighting it until I heard the Holy Spirit say, "You know you are going to stay in the valley much longer if you do not take up joy, because the joy of the Lord is your strength and you are going to need your strength to climb your mountain." Yikes! I did not want to stay in the valley one second longer than necessary, so I immediately started singing the children's song, "I've got joy, joy, joy, joy down in my heart. Where? Down in my heart, down in my heart to stay. And I'm so happy, so very happy; I've got the love of Jesus in my heart…" I did not know if those were the correct words to the song, but I sang them anyway and joy came instantly. As soon as I made the choice, joy came! I intentionally traded a spirit of fainting for a mantle of praise (Isaiah 61:3)! Thanks to the leading of the Holy Spirit, I was able to make the trade quickly! It was a wise trade. Look at what the Bible says in the book of Deuteronomy.

> **Because you did not serve the Lord your God**
> **with joy and a glad heart, for the abundance of**
> **all things; therefore you shall serve your enemies**
> whom the Lord will send against you, in hunger,
> in thirst, in nakedness, and in the lack of all
> things; and He will put an iron yoke on your neck
> until He has destroyed you.
> —Deuteronomy 28:47-48

Not only will we be unable to climb our mountains without joy, but sadness and depression open a gateway to the enemy! However, joy will save our souls!

> Though you have not seen Him, you love Him,
> and though you do not see Him now, but believe
> in Him, **you greatly rejoice with joy inexpressible**
> **and full of glory, obtaining as the outcome of**
> **your faith the salvation of your souls.**
> —1 Peter 1:8-9

Wow, the promise for choosing joy is the salvation of our souls. Our souls include our mind, will and emotions! Jesus is the lover of our souls (Psalm 103)!

Righteous governmental influence comes through people who have their minds, wills and emotions aligned with the Holy Spirit. Joy is a force that can bring everything into balance. God's technologies are of a much higher form than the technologies of Sin. Mysteries and miracles are contained within God's Intellectual Properties and we can freely use them any time we want to!

Ultimately, God wants us to be joyful because He is joyful!

God Laughs!

During my prayer time one day, I asked the Lord something and then I started laughing out loud. I could not stop laughing. I would try to pray something else and a deep laughter would continue to rise from my spirit. I laughed and laughed; it lasted for quite a long time. I thought, good gracious, if my husband walks in he is going to think I have completely lost it! In the Lord's Presence, there is fullness of joy (Psalm 16:11)! I had the most awesome time of communion with the Holy Spirit that morning and I knew He had taken care of all my requests. His laughter brought the answers!

God is not sad. He is not worried. He is joyful and He is attracted to joyful people! As a matter of fact, laughter is warfare technology from the throne of God.

> Why are the nations in an uproar
> And the peoples devising a vain thing?
> The kings of the earth take their stand
> And the rulers take counsel together
> Against the Lord and against His Anointed,
> saying, "Let us tear their fetters apart
> And cast away their cords from us!"
> **He who sits in the heavens laughs,**
> The Lord scoffs at them.
> —Psalm 2:1-4

God has opponents just as we do and He uses laughter to destroy their opposing plans! If God uses laughter, don't you think it would be a good weapon for us to use as well? If the rulers of this world are counseling against you, the Lord's anointed, then you should laugh! If you need breakthrough in paying your bills, take your bills out and laugh! If you need breakthrough on a project, take it out and laugh! I know it sounds silly, but God's ways are higher than our ways (Isaiah 55:8-9) and His foolishness is wiser than man's greatest wisdom!

This foolish plan of God is wiser than the wisest of human plans, and God's weakness is stronger than the greatest of human strength.

—1 Corinthians 1:25 NLT

If God says to laugh when the enemy is plotting against us, then we should laugh! One day I had a few girlfriends over for a luncheon. I brought out a project that I was having difficulty with. I sat it down in front of us so we could pray. God told me to laugh, so I laughed by faith which turned into real, true laughter. The laughter brought in the glory cloud of the Lord and a mighty breakthrough came! God is attracted to laughter and joy!

Darkness can't comprehend His ways, but we can because we walk in His light. God has secret technologies for us. Laughter works; it is a holy technology from our Father in Heaven!

Anointed with Joy

Did you know that Jesus was anointed with joy more than all the others around Him?

You have loved righteousness and hated wickedness; Therefore God, **Your God, has anointed You with the oil of joy above Your fellows.**

—Psalm 45:7

We are the Bride of Christ and He is coming back for a Church without spot or wrinkle (Ephesians 5:27). A few of the spots and wrinkles He wants washed and ironed out are sadness, gloom, and depression. Those are not attractive to Him. The Kingdom of God is righteousness, peace, and joy in the Holy Spirit!

He wants us to rejoice in what He has already done for us! A merry heart does good for the soul just as medicine does good for the body. When our souls prosper our bodies prosper too

(Proverbs 17:22; 3 John 1-2)! Many times sicknesses latch on to weak places of the soul. Laughter brings healing to our souls and bodies!

**I will rejoice greatly in the Lord,
My soul will exult in my God;**
For He has clothed me with garments of salvation,
He has wrapped me with a robe of righteousness,
As a bridegroom decks himself with a garland,
And as a bride adorns herself with her jewels.
For as the earth brings forth its sprouts,
And as a garden causes the things sown in
it to spring up, **So the Lord God will cause
righteousness and praise to spring up before all
the nations.**
—Isaiah 61:10-11

My desire is that the Lord would use the information contained within the pages of this book to cause righteousness and praise to spring up in your life and before all the nations!

**When you win, we plan to raise the roof and
lead the parade with our banners. May all your
wishes come true!**
—Psalm 20:5 MSG

Judy Coventry

ENDNOTES

Definition: Trading Floor

1. "trading floor." Dictionary.com's 21st Century Lexicon. Dictionary.com, LLC. 17 Apr. 2014. <Dictionary.com http://dictionary.reference.com/browse/trading floor>.

Chapter 1: The Clash of Two Kingdoms

1. Intellectual property. (2014, April 16). In Wikipedia, The Free Encyclopedia. Retrieved 17:35, April 21, 2014, from http://en.wikipedia.org/w/index.php?title=Intellectual_property&oldid=604455686.

Chapter 5: Trading at the Gates

1. Ralph Gower, The New Manners and Customs of Bible Times (Chicago: Moody Press, 1987 and 2000), 150-151.

Chapter 7: The Threshing Floor – Pathway to Glory

1. S. Michael Houdmann, GotQuestions.Org, http://www.gotquestions.org/threshing-floor.html.

Chapter 9: Trading for a Lost Generation

1. Shareholder. (2014, April 7). In Wikipedia, The Free Encyclopedia. Retrieved 18:18, April 21, 2014, from http://en.wikipedia.org/w/index.php?title=Shareholder&oldid=603193730.

2. Dutch Sheets, Baal, (HAPN), http://www.hapn.us/Websites/oapn/Images/Resource%20docs/baal%20divorce/Baal%20-%20from%20Dutch%20Sheet's%20teaching%20-%20Feb%202010.pdf.

Chapter 12: Trade Winds from Heaven

1. Tradewind. (2014, March 21). In Wikipedia, The Free Encyclopedia. Retrieved 18:24, April 21, 2014, from http://en.wikipedia.org/w/index.php?title=Trade_wind&oldid=60064238

God has opponents just as we do and He uses laughter to destroy their opposing plans! If God uses laughter, don't you think it would be a good weapon for us to use as well?

A Note from the Author

A Note from the Author

A Note from the Author

A Note From the Author

If you have not heard the message of salvation I would like to share God's plan of redemption with you.

Religion versus Relationship

Let us revisit the two trees in the Garden of Eden: The Tree of the Knowledge of Good and Evil and the Tree of Life. One represents religion and the other relationship.

When Adam ate from the Tree of the Knowledge of Good and Evil, he made an unrighteous trade. He did not lose a religion, he lost a relationship. He lost his right standing with God and he also lost dominion over the earth. Instead of walking and talking with God in the cool of the day in Paradise as he did prior to eating from the tree's forbidden fruit, he hid himself from God when he heard His footsteps in the garden.

Sin's only motive is to separate us from God. Previous to the fall, Adam and Eve were clothed with the glory of God, with His Presence, but now they were naked and they knew it. God still wanted communion with Adam and Eve because He adored His creation. So, He sacrificed an animal to make clothes for them because without the shedding of blood there is no remission of sin (Hebrews 9:22). God wants to commune with man like He did with Adam and Eve in the garden. He created mankind for fellowship!

By the shedding of the animal's blood (Genesis 3), we can already see a picture of the shed blood of the Lord Jesus Christ, the Lamb of God who takes away the sin of the world (John 1:29).

God is the One who has made the biggest trade of all, His one and only Son, for the redemption of mankind. God expected a return on His investment: Restoration of relationship with mankind and salvation for all! That was His desire.

For God so loved the world that He gave His only begotten Son, that whoever believes in Him shall not perish, but have eternal life.

—John 3:16

God gave His one and only Son so that He could have many sons and daughters. Only the pure blood of a sinless Savior could blot out the sin of all mankind for all eternity. God was willing to give Jesus so He could gain us.

God's desire is relationship. Relationship comes from the Tree of Life, which represents the grace of the Lord Jesus Christ. God never desired religion. Religion comes from the Tree of the Knowledge of Good and Evil: Man makes up rules according to what he thinks is good and evil and expects God and man to follow his rules. That plan will never work because God's government is one of a kingdom not a democracy. In a kingdom there is only one person who sets the requirements and that is the king. The Kingdom of God is an absolute monarchy with a reigning King, Jesus Christ. His Word is law. His rule is absolutely sovereign. Jesus is the King of Kings and the Lord of Lords and every knee will bow and every tongue will confess that He is Lord to the glory of God the Father (Philippians 2:10).

When Jesus came to earth He never once preached religion. As a matter of fact, it was the religious crowd that crucified Him. He preached *"Repent, for the kingdom of heaven is at hand"* (Matthew 4:17).Jesus preached the Kingdom of God, never religion, and never denomination! He prayed, *"Our Father who is in Heaven, hallowed by Your name. **Your Kingdom come. Your will be done, on earth as it is in Heaven"*** (Matthew 6:9-10). He also prayed that we would be one, even as He and the Father are one (John 17:11).

The Kingdom of God is righteousness, peace and joy in the Holy Spirit (Romans 14:17), not a religion.

Religion is forbidden fruit from the Tree of the Knowledge of Good and Evil. Religion puts people in bondage to the rules of men. It blinds the hearts and minds of those who want to believe. It causes confusion. The Bible says that where there is confusion there is every evil work. Sin knew this and that is why religion was formed as part of Sin's Intellectual Property represented by the Tree of the Knowledge of Good and Evil.

God's ONLY requirement is that we believe in His Son Jesus Christ.

> **For God so loved the world that He gave His only begotten Son, that whoever believes in Him shall not perish, but have eternal life.** For God did not send the Son into the world to judge the world, but that the world might be saved through Him. He who believes in Him is not judged; he who does not believe has been judged already, because he has not believed in the name of the only begotten Son of God.
> —John 3:16-18

> Jesus said to him, "I am the way, and the truth and the life; **no one comes to the Father but through Me."**
> —John 14:6

We will never find God through religion. We can only find Him through relationship with Jesus Christ His only Son. God gave Jesus so He could gain YOU because He loves YOU and wants relationship with YOU. No strings attached, YOU, just the way YOU are!

God loves mankind and His desire is that none would perish. The Bible says that all have sinned and have fallen short of the glory of God; everyone needs a savior (Romans 3:23). We will never be saved by works; salvation is a gift. That was God's plan and He makes all the rules!

Religion wants us to work for our salvation, but God says that it is free. We just have to believe in His Son.

For by grace you have been saved through faith;
and that not of yourselves, **it is the gift of God;
not as a result of works, so that no one may
boast.**

—Ephesians 2:8

The Bible says that if we confess with our mouths and believe in our hearts that Jesus is Lord and that God raised Him from the dead we will be saved. That is the simplicity of the Gospel!

But what does it say? "The word is near you,
in your mouth and in your heart"—that is, the
word of faith which we are preaching, **that if you
confess with your mouth Jesus as Lord, and
believe in your heart that God raised Him from
the dead, you will be saved; for with the heart
a person believes, resulting in righteousness,
and with the mouth he confesses, resulting in
salvation.**

—Romans 10:8-10

If you would like to receive Jesus Christ as your Lord and Savior, please say this prayer:

Jesus, I believe that You are the Son of God and that You were sent from God the Father to die on the cross for my sins. Please forgive me for all of my sins and cleanse me from everything that separates me from God. I receive all that Your death, burial and resurrection purchased for me. Come into my heart and be my personal Lord and Savior. Fill me with Your Holy Spirit and make everything in my life brand new. Amen.

Therefore if anyone is in Christ, he is a new
creature; the old things passed away; behold,
new things have come.

—2 Corinthians 5:17

If you just prayed this prayer, it is important that you tell someone. My husband Andy and I would love to hear from you!

> "And I say to you, everyone who confesses Me
> before men, the Son of Man will confess him also
> before the angels of God."
>
> —Luke 12:8

Remember, God loves you and He has a big plan for your life!

Please email us: judy@mercytriumphsworldwide.com

CONTACT THE AUTHOR

Judy Coventry
Mercy Triumphs Worldwide
Email: judy@mercytriumphsworldwide.com

15741837R00144

Made in the USA
Middletown, DE
21 November 2014